Foreword

Dear Reader,

We have scanned the country and brought together the collective wisdom and expertise of transportation professionals implementing Intelligent Transportation Systems (ITS) projects across the United States. This information will prove helpful as you set out to plan, design, and deploy ITS in your communities.

This document is one in a series of products designed to help you provide ITS solutions that meet your local and regional transportation needs. The series contains a variety of formats to communicate with people at various levels within your organization and among your community stakeholders:

- **Benefits Brochures** let experienced community leaders explain in their own words how specific ITS technologies have benefited their areas;

- **Cross-Cutting Studies** examine various ITS approaches that can be taken to meet your community's goals;

- **Case Studies** provide in-depth coverage of specific approaches taken in real-life communities across the United States; and

- **Implementation Guides** serve as "how to" manuals to assist your project staff in the technical details of implementing ITS.

ITS has matured to the point that you are not alone as you move toward deployment. We have gained experience and are committed to providing our state and local partners with the knowledge they need to lead their communities into the next century.

The inside back cover contains details on the documents in this series, as well as sources to obtain additional information. We hope you find these documents useful tools for making important transportation infrastructure decisions.

Christine M. Johnson
Program Manager, Operations
Director, ITS Joint Program Office
Federal Highway Administration

Edward L. Thomas
Associate Administrator for
Research, Demonstration and
Innovation
Federal Transit Administration

NOTICE

The United States Government does not endorse products or manufacturers. Trademarks or manufacturers' names appear herein only because they are considered essential to the objective of this document.

Table of Contents

Executive Summary		*es-1*
Part 1:	*Introduction*	*1-1*
	Objective	*1-3*
	Methodology	*1-3*
Part 2:	*Incident Management Overview*	*2-1*
Part 3:	*The Case for an Incident Management Program*	*3-1*
	Problems Addressed by Incident Management	*3-1*
	What Incident Management Can Accomplish	*3-2*
Part 4:	*An Institutional Framework for Incident Management*	*4-1*
	Who Is Involved and How?	*4-1*
Part 5:	*Implementing an Incident Management Program*	*5-1*
	Following an Organized Framework	*5-1*
	Phase I: Program Concept	*5-2*
	Phase II: Program Development	*5-13*
	Phase III: Program Maintenance and Sustainability	*5-19*
Part 6:	*Lessons Learned in Implementing and Sustaining Incident Management Programs*	*6-1*
Conclusion		*7-1*
Appendix A:	*Incident Management Program Monitoring, Evaluation, and Reporting of Benefits/Influence*	*A-1*
Acknowledgements		
References		

List of Figures

Figure 1	*Timeline of Elements in Incident Management Process*	*2-1*
Figure 2	*Effect of Demand Reduction in Delays Caused by Incidents*	*3-2*
Figure 3	*A Framework for Organizing and Sustaining Incident Management Programs*	*5-3*
Figure A-1	*Sample Evaluation Goals and Objectives Table*	*A-1*
Figure A-2	*Sample Questionnaire*	*A-2*
Figure A-3	*Sample Table for Analysis of Data*	*A-3*
Figure A-4	*Sample Implementation of Recommendations Timeline*	*A-3*

Executive Summary

The purpose of this document is to assist organizations and their leaders in implementing and sustaining regional traffic incident management programs, both by examining some successful models, and by considering some of the lessons learned by early implementers. There is some form of incident management activity in most major and many mid-sized urban areas. Typically this involves each agency carrying out its own responsibilities, with primarily working-level and middle-management administrative teams to provide coordination with the other agencies who are also involved in their own aspects of managing incidents. Such a situation not only achieves less than the full potential benefit, but also leaves open many risks for failure within individual agencies or on a broader scale.

The objective of this document is to present a framework for developing what is missing in almost every urban area—a formal multiagency traffic incident management program, with endorsement by, participation from, and coordination by senior agency management, and which includes all of the participating agencies. Formalizing the incident management effort—turning it into an incident management program—involves such steps as developing a written and endorsed strategy and a plan to implement the strategy; identifying and building support from a full complement of stakeholders and with the public; gaining support and ongoing participation in program direction from agency senior executives; documenting the respective roles and responsibilities of participants; establishing program goals and objectives and evaluating performance on these; establishing incident management as a major mission within and between the participating agencies; and "mainstreaming" of funding for incident management into the traditional transportation planning process.

More importantly, formalizing the program transitions incident management from reliance on the cooperative relationships existing between responders and between middle management of the agencies to an official recognition and endorsement of incident management as a core agency activity at senior executive levels. Incident management is then recognized as an overall initiative and purpose within and across agencies, significantly increasing the likelihood that its influence will be recognized when policies and other programs which may impact it are being discussed. When incident management reaches program status, it starts to be integrated into every aspect of what each participating agency does, whether this is planning for its information technology needs, or defining the types of vehicles that the law enforcement agency acquires.

Similarly, such focus demonstrates a long-term commitment to incident management. Formalization moves incident management from "special program" status, subject to availability of resources from outside the mainstream, and places it into the category occupied by the ongoing missions of each agency, whose existence is not questioned at each budget and staffing cycle. It has a clearly defined strategy, linked to the regional and statewide strategies guiding such major areas as law enforcement and transportation. The

Executive Summary

strategy sets direction for incident management, supporting the policy and resource needs which increase its impact and effectiveness.

This program then also becomes a component in the budget process of each participating agency to obtain the resources needed to implement and sustain the program. This executive endorsement (and ongoing support and participation), as well as the infiltration of incident management into every major aspect of each agency, provides a foundation that sustains incident management from year to year across personnel changes and even political changes. Furthermore, it creates conditions where agencies support one another's requests for the resources necessary to carry out their respective incident management duties and for the resources to expand program scope and coverage.

This document begins by presenting the case for incident management, describing the extent of the impact of incidents in the United States and how this impact occurs. It then discusses goals, objectives, and potential benefits of formal incident management programs.

The primary goals of traffic incident management are to minimize the impact of incidents and reduce the probability of secondary incidents. Five measurable objectives of incident management are:

- Reducing the time for incident detection and verification
- Reducing response time (the time for response personnel and equipment to arrive at the scene)
- Exercising proper and safe on-scene management of personnel and equipment, while keeping as many lanes open to traffic as possible
- Reducing clearance time (the time required for the incident to be removed from the roadway)
- Providing timely, accurate information to the public that enables them to make informed choices.

This document provides a framework and a series of steps for implementing and sustaining a regional traffic incident management program. The framework involves:

Program Concept

- Describe the current state of incident management efforts
- Describe and justify formalizing incident management
- Identify stakeholders involved
- Develop program goals and objectives
- Identify institutional and jurisdictional challenges.

Program Development

- Obtain buy-in from stakeholders
- Develop performance measures for objectives
- Develop incident management program strategy and plan.

Program Maintenance and Sustainability

- Solidify relationships with stakeholders
- Evaluate performance against every objective
- Modify implementation strategy and plan based on evaluation
- Leverage public support.

The organizations typically involved in incident management are:

- Transportation agencies
- Law enforcement agencies
- Fire and rescue agencies (including emergency medical services)
- Hazardous materials (HAZMAT) cleanup services
- Towing and recovery companies
- Public and private traveler information providers
- Other public and private entities on an as-needed basis.

This document also provides a series of lessons learned from traffic incident management programs around the country. Finally, the document discusses the importance of program monitoring, evaluation and reporting, as well as the need for strategic planning throughout the process.

The intended audience for this document is mid- and upper-level managers in police, fire and emergency medical service departments, as well as transit and transportation agencies.

Part 1: Introduction

It has been estimated that 57 percent of the nation's traffic congestion is due to crashes and other incidents, amounting to 2.45 billion vehicle-hours of delay in 1997 in the 68 areas studied by the Texas Transportation Institute for their 1999 Urban Mobility Report. Between 10 and 20 percent of incidents are caused by other, pre-existing incidents.[1] In 1995, 10,200 police cars, 1,800 fire vehicles, and 2,900 ambulances were themselves involved in motor vehicle crashes.[2] With this type of impact on the health and well being of the nation and its citizens, a mandate exists in many areas to mitigate, to the extent possible, the impact of incidents on American roadways.

Organized traffic incident management is the primary tool in mitigating the impact. Traffic incident management involves multi-agency, multi-jurisdictional responses to traffic disruptions that result in congestion. Efficient management and coordination of these responses is essential to reducing the negative impact of incidents on safety and traffic flow, but coordinating the different agencies and jurisdictions can be challenging, given their diverse institutional functions and individual agency goals.

The results of effective incident management activity can be impressive:

- On the Gowanus/Prospect Expressway in Brooklyn, NY, the average time to clear all types of incidents was reduced 66 percent, from 1 1/2 hours to 31 minutes.

- Philadelphia's Traffic and Incident Management System (TIMS) has decreased freeway incidents by 40 percent, and reduced freeway closure time by 55 percent.

- San Antonio's TransGuide traffic management program reduced crashes by 35 percent, and secondary crashes by 30 percent on its urban freeways.

- Maryland reports a benefit/cost ratio of 5.6:1 for its Chesapeake Highway Advisories Routing Traffic incident management program, with a savings of 2 million vehicle-hours of delay per year from incident-related congestion.

- In Atlanta, the maximum time from incident verification to lane clearance was cut from 6 1/4 hours to 1 1/2 hours, resulting in an estimated decrease of 2 million vehicle-hours of delay per year.[3]

Although safety benefits of incident management are of equal importance, data on these are not readily available. These benefits would accrue from lower exposure risk and shorter periods of exposure for incident responders and incident victims, and fewer injuries to motorists resulting from the reduced number and severity of secondary incidents.

---

1 *Strategic Plan for IVHS in the United States, ITS America, 1992*
2 *Speech by Deputy Secretary of Transportation Mortimer Downey, April 19, 1999*
3 *Intelligent Transportation Systems Benefits: 1999 Update, Mitretek for USDOT, 1999*

Introduction

Typically, traffic incident management activity is underway in large- and medium-sized urban areas with significant traffic congestion problems. In order to be successful, incident management requires support from multiple organizations in the region that have a stake in responding to traffic incidents. Key to the success is a high level of interagency coordination, particularly among the state and local departments of transportation (DOT), state and local law enforcement agencies, fire departments, towing and recovery companies, HAZMAT cleanup companies, and other organizations that own, operate, report on, or are involved with transportation infrastructure. These include transit agencies, the media, local environmental protection agencies, insurance companies, and national agencies such as the National Transportation Safety Board or the Bureau of Alcohol, Tobacco, and Firearms.

Incident Management is not the core purpose of any response agency. Incident management coordination is usually initiated by individual agency champions who decide that agencies can do the job of incident clearance more effectively by working together more closely. Sometimes it is only one dynamic person who holds the effort together by force of personality, people skills, and aggressive decision-making which gains the respect of other players. The individual agency resources needed are provided to the extent that the mid-level managers can command them, but since incident management is not a core function of an agency, these resources are subject to being redirected, especially if the agency champion leaves.

Today's best incident programs have developed from small beginnings under the leadership of self-styled champions (from one or two agencies) who have rallied the support of their peers in partner agencies. These programs faced considerable difficulties in the beginning and consolidated their position later when the benefits to the community became clear.

Despite their success, incident management efforts are vulnerable to decline or demise for a number of reasons:

- Incident management is not viewed by most of the participating agencies as their primary role.

- Incident management requires involvement and commitment from multiple levels and departments within many of the participating agencies, adding to the challenge of building unified support due to the diversity of goals and personalities involved.

- The retirement of the original champions has left a number of incident management efforts without strong leaders capable of garnering sufficient fiscal and staffing resources.

- Most incident management efforts do not justify their existence with well-documented evaluations, leaving them vulnerable to budget cuts.

- Most incident management activity depends heavily on the operations and maintenance budgets of their state DOTs and may need to draw upon capital budgets of participating law enforcement and emergency services agencies.

Regional Traffic Incident Management Programs

In many locations, this funding must be re-approved annually and is not guaranteed.

- Since the senior executive leadership of many of the participating agencies is not always aware of the incident management effort's focus and needs, the effort may suffer budget cuts when money is tight.

Creating and maintaining effective, trust-based working relationships among the multitude of individuals and organizations involved in traffic incident management can be challenging. Equally challenging is the process of justifying both initial and ongoing investments in resources to support traffic incident management.

Traffic incident management is commonly classified as a category within the larger incident management arena. The effective multi-agency and multi-disciplinary management of traffic incidents is the focus of this report. It is recognized that the term 'incident management' has also been used to describe nationally-recognized protocol for on-site command and control procedures synonymous with 'incident command'. For the remainder of the document, references to incident management are intended to pertain to collective and cooperative practices used to effectively manage traffic incidents.

Objective

The objective of this implementation guide is to provide a robust framework for agencies to use to organize and conduct current and future incident management efforts, and to evolve these efforts into formal long-term sustained programs. Such a framework will help programs to grow in a structured manner, thus fostering sustainability and enhancing program performance and efficiency. The framework is not intended to imply that program evolution is necessarily a smooth progression with clear delineations from one step to the next, but rather to provide a list of activities which have been found to be important to successful transition from a cooperative effort to a sustainable program, and to provide a sense of the order in which such transition normally occurs. The framework is focused on the needs of mid-level managers and supervisors who often originate, have been tasked to implement, or are fostering continued operation and improvement of existing incident management efforts.

Methodology

While no single approach can be prescribed for all incident management efforts, a flexible framework based on experiences from successful incident management programs in the United States can be considered a highly effective approach to building a successful program. Thus, this guide will provide a multi-phase framework to organize and sustain successful incident management programs. This guide will also provide experiences based on actual cases from some of the most successful programs. It begins by introducing incident management and by describing why agencies involved in transportation should be interested in

Introduction

incident management, as well as what they may reasonably expect as the benefits of effective incident management. This guide then describes an overall plan for implementing and operating regional incident management, and gives details of each step in the plan, within the context of the institutional framework. The guide also provides both lessons learned and examples from several nationally recognized incident management programs. Following the document's conclusion, the reader will find appendices containing more detail on several aspects of the process described earlier, and a list of relevant reference documents.

This implementation guide is based on face-to-face interviews with incident management leaders in Atlanta, Houston, Maryland, Seattle, Milwaukee, Chicago, Los Angeles, San Francisco, Detroit, and San Antonio. Information was also gathered through an extensive review of literature about and from incident management efforts nationwide. This information was then combined with business management best practices to develop this guide. All efforts were coordinated through and reviewed by Mr. David Helman of the Federal Highway Administration Office of Travel Management and Dr. Joseph Peters of the ITS Joint Program Office, without whose assistance and guidance the document could not have been prepared.

Part 2: Incident Management Overview

For the purpose of this guide, traffic incident management is defined as:

> An operational strategy for a transportation network that involves a coordinated and planned inter-jurisdictional, cross-functional, multidisciplinary, and ongoing approach to restore traffic to normal conditions after an incident occurs, and to minimize the delay caused by the resulting disruption to traffic flow.

Traffic incident management involves the systematic use of human and mechanical processes for:

- Quickly detecting, verifying, and clearing temporary obstructions on roadways in a specific operational area
- Providing information about such obstructions to the traveling public
- Restoring normal traffic flow as efficiently and safely as possible
- Providing multi-agency, multi-disciplinary frameworks for planning, conducting and evaluating special events that significantly impact the transportation system.

Effective incident management encompasses six basic elements or steps, often overlapping, as illustrated.

Figure 1: Timeline of Elements in the Incident Management Process

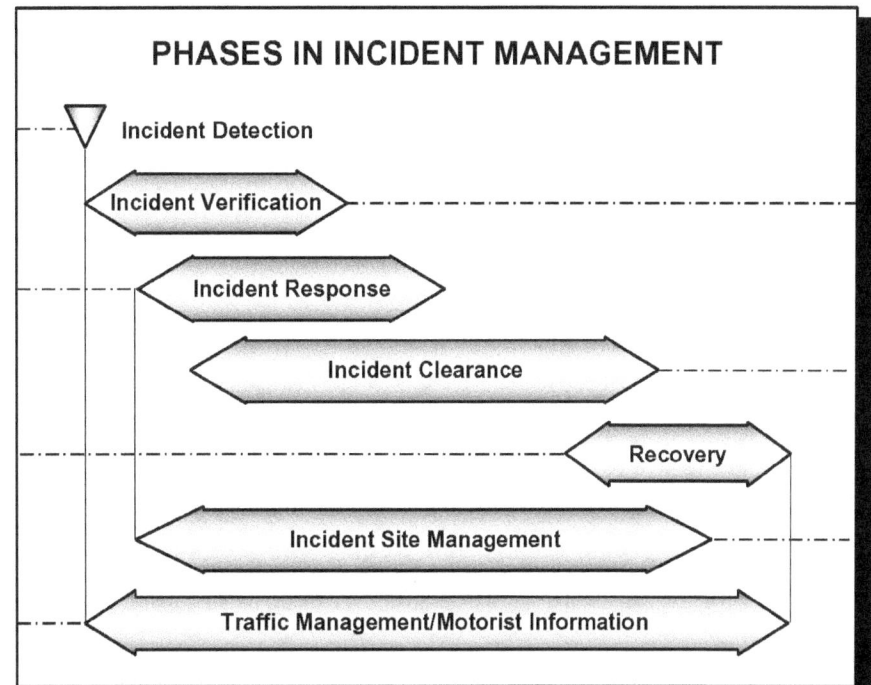

Part 3: The Case for Incident Management

Incidents on the road network can have a significant impact on the lives of citizens and on the economic health of communities. Effective management of traffic incidents can help to mitigate their impact.

Problems Addressed by Incident Management

Two important ways that effective management of traffic incidents can mitigate the incident impact are:

- By promoting rapid, well organized and coordinated clearance of incidents, thus improving safety of responders, victims, and the motoring public
- By reducing the impact of the incident on regional travel and travelers.

The incident scene is a complex and dangerous environment. It exposes both victims and responders to any combination of moving traffic, hazardous materials, fire and electrical hazards, damaged vehicles and debris, and stressful weather conditions. Any safe and coordinated actions that can be taken to reduce the length of exposure and safely control the scene have a direct benefit. Coordinated incident management—where organizations work together to accomplish their respective duties as quickly as possible—and where each takes measures that facilitate (or at least do not impede) the actions of other responders—is a major step beyond each agency simply performing its duties without close coordination with the other participants. Actions that reduce the traffic hazard, such as properly established lane closures and diversions and provision of traveler information, also decrease the latent traffic demand. The number of secondary incidents which then also require attention from responders is effectively reduced.

Congestion resulting from traffic crashes and other incidents, or *non-recurrent* congestion, is one of the most significant elements in most metropolitan areas' congestion problem. The occurrence of an incident in a transportation system disrupts traffic flow and temporarily reduces roadway capacity. Incidents intensify the impact of recurrent congestion during peak periods, sometimes even as a result of incidents that occurred during off-peak periods.

The effects of an incident on a facility's normal traffic flow are illustrated in Figure 2. When an incident occurs, highway capacity is reduced and traffic queues begin to build. The vehicle hours of delay accrued by motorists in the queue are represented by the shaded area between the normal flow rate and the incident flow rate—the difference between traffic demand and available road capacity at the incident location. If traffic demand going toward the incident site is reduced by diverting traffic to alternate routes, the delay will be minimized (dark gray area, noted as Cumulative Delay with Demand Reduction). However, if traffic is not diverted, additional delay will accrue (shaded area). Upon incident clearance, traffic will clear through the incident site until the queue is dissipated. Nevertheless, the getaway traffic flow will be limited by the maximum capacity of the highway.

The Case for Incident Management

Incident management helps relieve congestion by reducing the impact of incidents on traffic in two ways: by reducing incident detection, response, and clearance times; and by disseminating information that advises drivers to use alternate routes, thus shortening the queue.

Figure 2: Effect of Demand Reduction in Delays Caused by Incidents

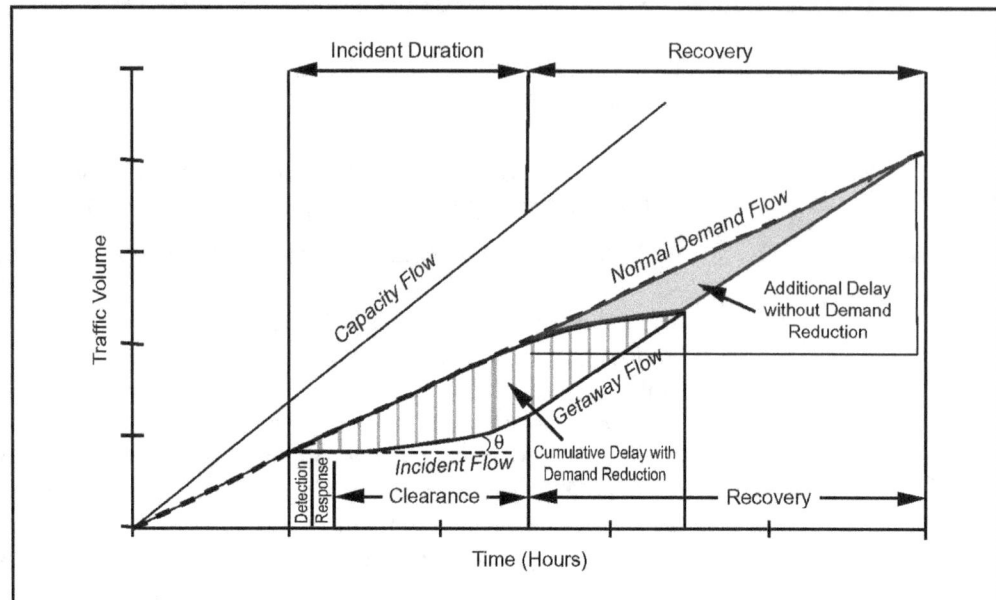

(Incident Management: "Challenges, Strategies, and Solutions for Advancing Safety and Roadway Efficiency" Final Technical Report. ATA Foundation and Cambridge Systematics, 1997)

What Incident Management Can Accomplish

The overall goals of incident management are to minimize the impact of incidents and reduce the probability of secondary incidents. Five measurable objectives of incident management are:

- Reducing the time for incident detection and verification
- Reducing response time (the time for response personnel and equipment to arrive at the scene)
- Exercising proper and safe on-scene management of personnel and equipment, while keeping as many lanes open to traffic as possible
- Reducing clearance time (the time required for the incident to be removed from the roadway)
- Providing timely, accurate information to the public that enables them to make informed choices, such as revising travel plans and using alternate routes.

When achieved, these combined objectives reduce the overall delay incurred by travelers using the road network and improve the overall safety of both incident victims and responders. At a societal level, this translates into gains in economic productivity, reduced fuel consumption and air pollution, and increased on-time delivery of goods and services to businesses and consumers.

Part 4: An Institutional Framework for Incident Management

Who Is Involved and How?

Coordinating and managing responses to an incident by multiple agencies and jurisdictions requires a complex array of interagency relationships, and relationships between key incident management personnel at those agencies. These relationships form the basis for the institutional framework of an incident management program, and in most cases must exist before a formal framework can be undertaken.

The organizations that are typically involved with most incidents are:

- **Law Enforcement Agencies**—These include state, county, and city police departments responsible for public safety and enforcement, who respond to traffic incidents on the interstate system, state roads, and city streets. Law enforcement agencies are often the first to receive notice of an incident (as receiver of 911 calls) or the first to detect incidents because of their role in traffic patrol and traffic law enforcement. They are typically in command at the incident scene, may execute traffic control measures at the scene, request additional services, and lead crash investigations when the incident results in personal injuries, fatalities, or significant property damage.

- **Fire and Rescue Agencies**—These agencies include county, city, volunteer, and private fire and rescue organizations. They respond to incidents involving fire, hazardous materials, medical emergencies, life support, or rescue, and thus play an important role on incident management teams. Though fire and rescue agencies respond to fewer than 15 percent of all incidents occurring on freeways[4], their support during incident response and clearance is critical for the efficient movement of traffic at a scene. Due to the organizational structure of fire companies, and their primary focus on public safety and the safety of incident responders, coordinating operations with fire departments can present challenges. The best incident management efforts have a high level of coordination with their fire and rescue departments through involved planning and education of each other's staff. This has led to an appreciation that more rapid and coordinated incident response cuts response operation time, and therefore reduces the period during which response personnel and crash victims are exposed to the hazards presented by adjacent traffic.

- **Transportation Agencies**—These include departments of transportation and other agencies that operate and maintain the road network in the region, including state DOTs, city and county public works departments, and others. These agencies generally provide traffic management support, incident information dissemination to other impacted organizations, equipment and

---

[4] Incident Management: Challenges, Strategies, and Solutions for Advancing Safety and Roadway Efficiency" Final Technical Report. ATA Foundation and Cambridge Systematics, 1997

personnel for incident clearance, special signing, activation of detours, containment of minor hazardous materials spills, debris removal, and related activities.

- **Hazardous Materials Cleanup Services**—These services are generally provided by private companies, although for small situations, other responding agencies such as DOT Maintenance or the service patrol may perform cleanup. While fire departments often have HAZMAT containment capability, they usually rely on private companies under contract for HAZMAT cleanup. Highly unusual payloads may require specialized assistance, as was the case in 1999 with an overturned gunpowder truck at a major interchange on the Washington, D.C. highway network. Significant spills may involve not only the HAZMAT service, but also related environmental protection authorities.

- **Towing and Recovery Companies**—These are private companies that provide towing and recovery services for highway incidents. They are often under contract to one of the agencies involved in incident management, may independently patrol the roadways, or may have been contacted by the motorist. Special recovery resources, such as heavy lift or rotator vehicles, are usually privately contracted for by an involved agency.

- **Public and Private Traveler Information Providers**—These include public agencies and private companies such as information service providers (ISP) that collect, process, and disseminate traffic and transport-related information to benefit travelers. Common methods to disseminate information are television, radio, the Internet, highway advisory radio, and variable message signs.

- **Transit Agencies**—These include bus, subway, and commuter rail companies, both public and private. Buses are frequently affected by traffic delays resulting from incidents. Transit can also reduce congestion caused by long-duration incidents by providing a transportation alternative. Information must be passed on to transit agencies in order for them to make proper operational decisions in response to an incident, and to ISPs so that information is provided to the public on availability of transit alternatives. Transit buses, by their constant presence on the road network, can also serve as "traffic probes", reporting back information about potential and actual problems much earlier than it would otherwise reach the Transportation Management Center (TMC).

The magnitude or nature of an incident may require other organizations to respond to or participate in incident management on an as-needed basis.

In working with incident management partners, it is important first to recognize and then work through differences in organizational culture.

- Some organizations operate around-the-clock, and are response-oriented, while others are not.
- Police officers are trained to act autonomously, assume command, and make unilateral decisions, whereas fire and rescue personnel act in teams.
- Private sector organizations like towing companies are profit-driven and therefore very mindful of the amount of time they are involved and the resources they apply.

- Media often view an incident primarily for its relative newsworthiness, and may not give adequate consideration to additional information from which travelers could benefit.

The impact of major traffic incidents transcends political, jurisdictional, and geographical boundaries, and may affect entire regional road networks and hundreds of thousands of travelers. For those reasons, it is important to coordinate response regionally rather than just locally. Often, agencies across jurisdictions can share information about how to address specific incident management situations, allowing agencies to benefit from the experience of outside partner organizations.

Such coordination must take place at more than one organizational level. The traditional relationships for managing incidents have been at supervisory and working levels, often on an informal basis, and between the middle managers sponsoring the incident management coordination. To achieve true success in institutionalizing incident management programs, the highest organizational levels must also be involved and formally committed to the incident management program. Formation of a senior executive level steering committee to set direction for and oversee the work of other incident management related committees and staff is a direct way in which to focus efforts and increase the likelihood of a sustainable program. Maryland and Milwaukee have both made some progress in this area by instituting steering committees to lead their respective incident management programs, although neither steering committee has an extensive presence from the most senior agency levels.

Endorsement and involvement at senior executive levels facilitates the filtering of incident management issues and concerns throughout each of the involved agencies. Thus, incident management considerations are reflected in policy discussions, staffing profiles, and budget preparation. Interagency cooperation extends beyond simple coordination to the level of each agency supporting the relevant budget line item applications of other participating agencies and of agencies identifying cooperative funding and budget opportunities such as application for special grants.

Undertaking incident management from a regional perspective is also key to creating a sustainable incident management program. This is particularly true in planning. Using a regional approach for incident management planning offers a number of opportunities by:

- Providing a predictable and consistently administered mechanism for bringing stakeholders together to address transportation operations and management issues of mutual concern, through the use of
  - A formal interorganizational structure
  - Regular, structured functions and meetings
- Promoting greater consideration of systems management and operations as part of a region's overall approach to meeting transportation needs

An Institutional Framework for Incident Management

- Allowing agencies to coordinate efforts and technologies such that future projects will be compatible, resulting in cost savings and easier integration of systems over time

- Facilitating agreement among agencies on future operational strategies and information exchanges to be pursued

- Providing an opportunity to coordinate long-term implementation of incident management programs and establish general strategies and priorities.

The coordination of this complex web of relationships requires that the functions, cultures, and objectives of each agency are well understood by all agencies involved, and that trust exists between the agencies and the individuals involved. Efficient coordination, shared objectives, and mutual understanding are key to minimizing conflicts and maximizing incident management performance.

Who's the Boss?: A Hypothetical Scenario at an Incident Scene

On a rainy evening during rush hour in Capital City, a tractor trailer carrying 40 tons of hazardous material goes over an embankment, landing on its side to the right of the roadway. The regional 911 center receives hundreds of calls from passing motorists with cellular phones. The local state patrol dispatch center, fire department, and HAZMAT center are contacted, and vehicles are dispatched to the scene. Based on the likelihood of a significant traffic problem, information on the suspected incident is also shared with the regional TMC. The TMC investigates with its closed circuit TV (CCTV), and directs a patrolling DOT safety service vehicle to the scene.

Upon arrival at the scene, the police officer begins diverting traffic away from the scene. The DOT service patrol officer sets up cones and flares, and activates the variable message sign on his truck to assist the officer in directing traffic.

The fire chief and engine arrive and park their vehicles across two additional lanes of the freeway in the interest of protecting the responders and travelers. Traffic grinds to a halt. Although the personnel at the scene can't see it, two fender benders occur in the rapidly forming queue of traffic, compounding the problem.

The police officer and fire chief engage in an extended discussion over how to manage the incident. The police officer, while concerned about public safety, has had more exposure to traffic control and recognizes the need to quickly and efficiently restore traffic conditions to avoid secondary crashes. The fire chief's highest priority is the safety of the crew at the scene and the parties injured in the crash and has yet to be convinced that adequate safety can be achieved through effective traffic control without establishing large safety zones.

Because of the difference in experiences between the responding agencies and lack of a common understanding of and approach to working together in such situations, the officer and fire chief are forced to work out their differences on site, delaying incident clearance, and further straining the relationships between the organizations.

Had the organizations established regular communications, developed coordinated procedures, participated in joint training activities, and built trust in their desires to achieve each agency's goals, this scenario might have been avoided.

Part 5: Implementing an Incident Management Program

Effective incident management requires a systematic and integrated approach that transcends jurisdictional boundaries. Therefore, the development of an incident management program must include a regional perspective that allows for the coordination of all its stakeholders and the crossing of jurisdictional boundaries. Such interagency coordination is not easily achieved. The primary barriers to developing regional incident management programs are institutional issues that must be overcome if an effective program is to be developed, implemented, and sustained.

This section provides an overview of the challenges to implementing a regional incident management program.

Following an Organized Institutional Framework

Most incident management programs have grown under the leadership of one or more partner agencies that typically invest a disproportionately high level of resources in incident management, particularly during the early stages. Without a predefined structure and organization, this approach can lead to differing expectations among the partners and result in strained relationships that take years to mend.

Formalized incident management programs are a logical next step from the everyday performance of incident-related duties by the agencies and personnel involved in managing incidents. Relationships are created, trust and understanding begin to grow, and processes begin to be refined. Often the value of formalizing the program is first recognized and promoted by middle management at the participating agencies and organizations. The task facing these managers is to raise the commitment to incident management to senior agency levels, and to build interagency links at these levels. Once senior participation begins, a strategy will be created which provides guidance and direction to the program, and which supports long term commitment of resources, and incorporation of incident management influence into every relevant policy or program decision.

Following an organized approach to formalizing the incident management program ensures clear expectations among the partners, resulting in increased cooperation and effectiveness. Such an approach includes clearly defining each agency's role and explaining how the agencies can most effectively work together. Following this approach, combined with tactics such as joint training exercises, after-action analyses, and regular and effective communication, will lead to increased trust and respect among partner agencies.

Due to the involvement of numerous agencies and jurisdictions, organizing an incident management program should follow a phased approach. The three-phased approach presented below can help provide the partners with sufficient structure to organize the numerous activities involved while allowing adequate flexibility to accommodate their unique situations. Activities are grouped into three phases, focusing on concept development, program development, and program maintenance and sustainability.

This framework is not intended to imply that programs can only be developed in an orderly, stepwise fashion with clearly defined points of demarcation between each stage. The more common model is one where incident management evolves, at varying rates, from initial, informal efforts driven by each agency's activities, roles, and responsibilities, to a formalized, documented, rehearsed, and clearly understood process which continues to improve as opportunities are identified and can be implemented. Often the progression to a formal program will encounter setbacks, and will have to repeat a step or will have to skip to a step further down the process in order to satisfy agency schedules or political demands. This will require continued focus on the primary goals and objectives, and flexibility to sustain the incident management activity even when the degree of progress toward formalization is discouraging.

The following framework is provided to assist incident management efforts in their progression, by identifying critical elements in evolution and providing some insight into possible approaches and issues.

Phase I: Program Concept

Developing a Program Concept document is the first step in incident management program formalization. The document focuses on the basic foundations of the incident management program. The document describes, based on current incident management activity, the idea of a formal incident management program. The document then justifies the need for and the benefits to be derived from having a formal incident management program. It is not enough to say that just because other places have successful incident management programs that a this area needs one as well. As with any program, the regional incident management program must be tailored to the needs, resources, capabilities, and priorities of the region and the participating organizations. The program will reflect the technical and institutional realities of the region's transportation network, authorities, and travel conditions.

The concept phase must be completed in a relatively short period. It is critical to get the program formalization started while the momentum of the partners is still high, and to keep the process moving forward with recognizable results. Spending too much time in defining the program concept could lead to withering of support, especially from senior managers of the partner agencies.

The typical steps in the Program Concept phase are:

- Describe the current state of incident management efforts
- Describe and justify formalizing incident management
- Identify the full range of stakeholders who should be involved
- Develop program goals and objectives
- Identify institutional and jurisdictional challenges.

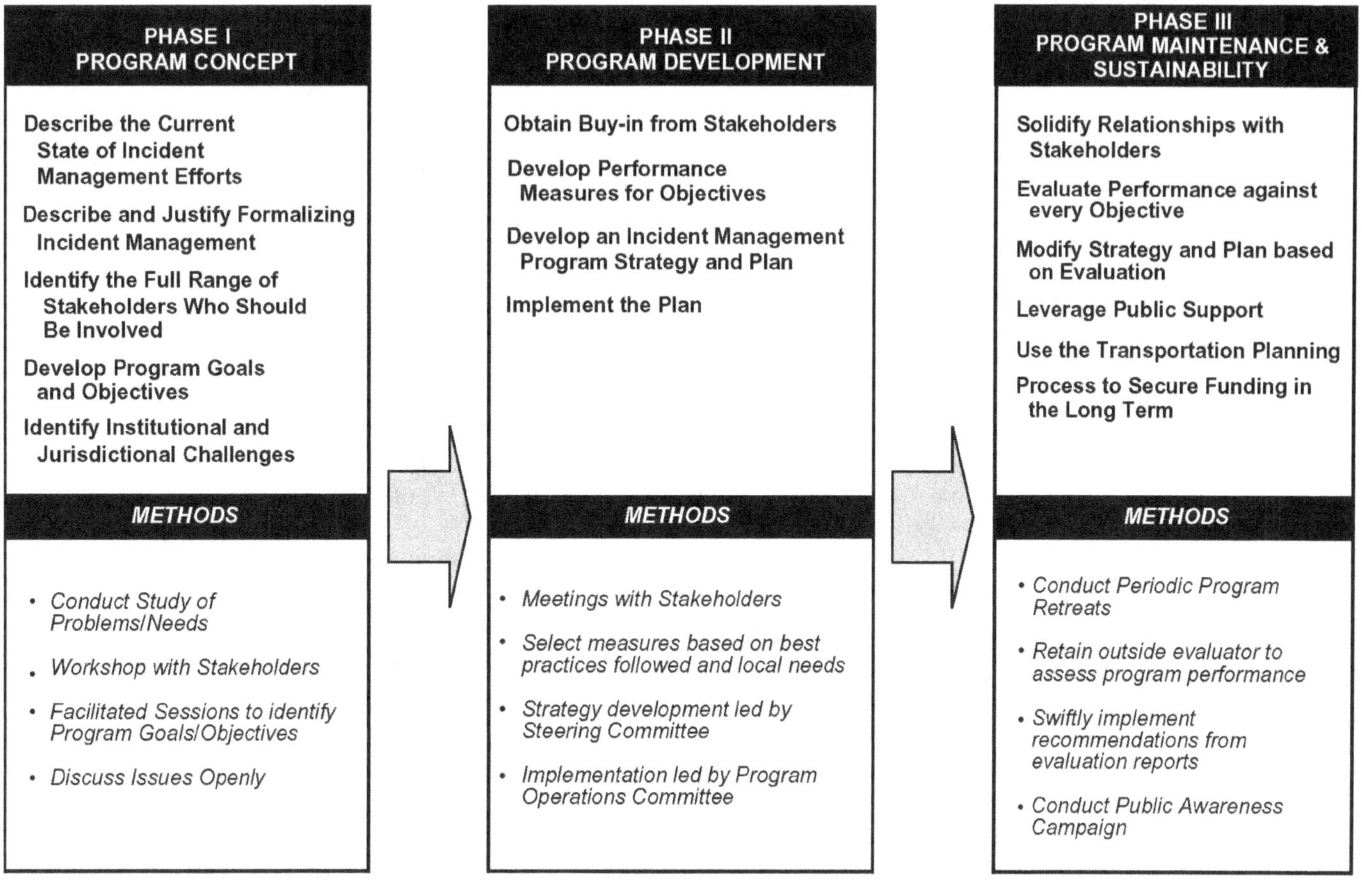

PHASE I PROGRAM CONCEPT	PHASE II PROGRAM DEVELOPMENT	PHASE III PROGRAM MAINTENANCE & SUSTAINABILITY
Describe the Current State of Incident Management Efforts Describe and Justify Formalizing Incident Management Identify the Full Range of Stakeholders Who Should Be Involved Develop Program Goals and Objectives Identify Institutional and Jurisdictional Challenges	Obtain Buy-in from Stakeholders Develop Performance Measures for Objectives Develop an Incident Management Program Strategy and Plan Implement the Plan	Solidify Relationships with Stakeholders Evaluate Performance against every Objective Modify Strategy and Plan based on Evaluation Leverage Public Support Use the Transportation Planning Process to Secure Funding in the Long Term
METHODS	*METHODS*	*METHODS*
• *Conduct Study of Problems/Needs* • *Workshop with Stakeholders* • *Facilitated Sessions to identify Program Goals/Objectives* • *Discuss Issues Openly*	• *Meetings with Stakeholders* • *Select measures based on best practices followed and local needs* • *Strategy development led by Steering Committee* • *Implementation led by Program Operations Committee*	• *Conduct Periodic Program Retreats* • *Retain outside evaluator to assess program performance* • *Swiftly implement recommendations from evaluation reports* • *Conduct Public Awareness Campaign*

Figure 3: A Framework for Organizing and Sustaining Incident Management Programs

Implementing an Incident Management Program

Describe The Current State Of Incident Management Efforts

The foundation of a formal incident management program is almost always the incident management activity already underway. Each agency or organization is typically carrying out its own idea of what its role is in dealing with incidents. Often, there is little formal coordination of these efforts between the agencies. At best, such existing coordination is based on relationships between responders, and between middle management in each of the responding agencies/organizations. Often such coordination was sparked by an unusual need, such as hosting a major sporting tournament, or by an embarrassing event which created temporary traffic havoc or which inconvenienced an influential person.

Within each agency incident management resources would typically be drawn from other, higher level line items, and thus would not clearly visible in the budgeting process. It would be unusual to find an identifiable budget line item for incident management. Similarly, there are seldom staff within each agency dedicated to formal incident management efforts. More commonly, there may be a person or two whose primary duties are to better coordinate response to traffic incidents with other agencies through organizing training and awareness, and by enabling some technical improvements to facilitate communication.

The objective of this step is to document what is already being done, so that the full scope of incident management can be understood, and so that the importance to each agency of sustaining incident management is clearly visible at the executive level. This step also highlights how many different aspects of each agency's operation are impacted by or can/should be involved in incident management.

Describe and Justify Formalizing Incident Management

At some point, one or more of the participants, often at the middle management level, realize that formalizing the effort into full program status will assist in many ways in improving and sustaining it. The next step is to create a vision of how the formalized incident management program may work, and to justify having a formal program.

There are two aspects to this next step: demonstrating the need for sustained incident management, and understanding the benefits that can be derived from formalizing incident management into program status. Since incident management addresses mitigation of non-recurrent congestion and the hazards of dealing with incidents, it is necessary to document the significance of non-recurrent congestion and incidents in order to justify formalizing the program. Potential sources of information include both state and local departments of transportation, the metropolitan planning organization (MPO), and state and local law enforcement agencies. Such impacts can often be quantified in terms of lost work days and general negative impact on productivity, property damage, air quality damage, and wasted fuel. Documenting the impact is best accomplished by conducting a short study. The impact of incident management activity elsewhere in areas comparable to the one under consideration can be used to predict the results. For example, in planning for a small/medium urban area with large rural environs, don't solicit results from a large metropolitan area. Such predictions should also be based on program implementation rates similar to that desired, i.e., gradual rollout or rapid implementation and expansion.

While it is important to make an effective case, it is also important not to oversell the potential benefits. Failure to achieve expected benefits will often lead to questions about the program's necessity, which will be difficult to answer satisfactorily.

The second aspect is to understand how a formal program is superior to an informal incident management effort. The most important reason is that a formal program is likely to survive and continue to operate under conditions (such as loss of a key champion, funding, or other resources) where an informal effort may disappear. In a similar sense, a formal program is able to justify the resources needed to expand, either functionally or geographically, or to respond to special circumstances such as a major multiyear roadway reconstruction effort. The effectiveness of incident management is also enhanced by formalization. In particular, once a program is endorsed by senior agency executives as a major initiative within and across agencies, its influence can be exercised as policies and programs are considered from which it can benefit. Thus, it becomes a component of every activity within an agency, and not just a special effort which must stand on its own.

It is also important to understand to whom the program should be justified, and what factors and issues are important to these key decision makers. The most important decision makers are those whose organizations would be the primary participants, who have relevant responsibilities, and who have funding or other resources available. It will, however, be necessary to justify the program at more than one level of an agency or organization, depending on the commitment or support which will be required. The justification must also speak to each organization's and each level's most important goals and concerns. It may be useful to produce a series of documents targeted at different audiences to justify the program. Key stakeholders, in turn, can use these documents to generate additional support within their organizations. The multilevel structure of USDOT's information and assistance program series on incident management may serve as a model:

- Tri-fold brochures with peer comments and benefits emphasis targeted at senior agency executives, and potentially to elected officials:

  Improved Mobility, Saving Lives—Safety Service Patrols, EDL# 6872

  Safer Travel, Improved Economic Productivity—Incident Management Systems, EDL# 6868

  Sharing Resources, Coordinating Response—Deploying and Operating Incident Management Systems, EDL# 6869

- A 26-page "cross-cutting" study of benefits, lessons learned, and successful practices:

  Incident Management Successful Practices—A Cross-Cutting Study, EDL# 11484

- This document, a 50-page implementation guide with step-by-step instructions and detailed appendices for some topics targeted at implementing managers:

  Regional Traffic Incident Management Programs Implementation Guide, EDL# 13149

- A 175-page handbook of practices and procedures targeted at day-to-day supervisors—an update to the 1991 document *The Freeway Incident Management Handbook:*

  Traffic Incident Management Handbook, EDL# 13285

- 2-day course on implementing incident management, including binders of course and reference material (National Highway Institute Course No. 13348)

- National Incident Management Coalition half-day workshops for elected officials and senior agency executives

The documents listed above are available through the USDOT Electronic Document Library (EDL) at http://www.its.dot.gov/welcome.htm. More information about the National Highway Institute courses is available at http://www.nhi.fhwa.dot.gov.

Regional Traffic Incident Management Programs

Maryland's Incident Management Program Begins at the Beach

As in other vacationer corridors, Marylanders stream to the beach on summer weekends. Maryland State Highway Administration (MdSHA) implemented a multifaceted program of outreach, traveler information, traffic management, roadway improvements, and incident management, titled "Reach the Beach", to assist motorists journeying to and from the shore. The program was both successful and highly popular with Maryland citizens, and cast MdSHA in a very positive light. Based on this experience, and recognizing the potential for such a program in other areas of the state experiencing increasing traffic demand, MdSHA created a program—Chesapeake Highway Advisories Routing Traffic (CHART)—to provide incident management statewide. As a component of CHART, Maryland became one of the first states to pass "push off" legislation allowing state vehicles to move disabled or abandoned vehicles from active lanes at incident scenes, and has equipped many MdSHA and Maryland State Patrol vehicles with push-off bumpers. MdSHA also automatically dispatches a front-end loader and a sand truck to any incident involving a truck. If first responders see that this equipment is not needed, it is turned around enroute and sent back. Experience, however, dictates that these pieces of equipment are often needed for truck accidents and in the past were difficult to get to the scene quickly. The acronym CHART has since been renamed to stand for "Coordinated Highways Action Response Team" to reflect the expanded statewide nature of the program.

Incident Management In Milwaukee Begins With MPO Support

The recommendations in a regional transportation plan developed in the mid-1970s were carried forward into a preliminary detailed plan which was completed in the mid-1980s. A joint study conducted by the regional planning committee and Wisconsin DOT (WisDOT) included local law enforcement. The result of the study process was consensus about having a central TMC, areawide ramp meters with High Occupancy Vehicle (HOV) preferential access, and incident management and traveler information elements of traffic management. The incident management recommendation included recognition of the significant impact of any incident on typical flow conditions. The study concluded that the regional incident management program needed to quickly identify, confirm, and remove atypical conditions. Previously, incidents were identified to law enforcement, but not confirmed until an officer was on the scene, and no action to clear was taken until ordered by the officer on scene. This study provided the foundation for the MONITOR system and the area's incident management program.

Implementing an Incident Management Program

Identify the Full Range of Stakeholders Who Should Be Involved

Once the need for a formalized incident management program is understood and the benefit is clearly expressed, other affected stakeholders have to be identified. Up to this point, the program's focus has been on the primary participants at working and perhaps middle management levels. Numerous additional agencies (and possibly private sector organizations) and jurisdictions may play a role in responding to the full range of incidents in any urban area. From this group, a core set of key officials at primary stakeholder agencies has to be identified as the most active program partners. These core stakeholders will be involved in guiding the program. A second group of stakeholders, who will participate on an as-needed basis for special events and emergency response planning, also has to be identified and appropriately involved. Also, within this tier of stakeholders will be other departments within the primary stakeholder agencies, who have lesser involvement in daily incident management activity, but whose input and support will be critical to having a successful program.

The organizations listed for Milwaukee's incident management program can serve as a starting point. Since a regional approach is necessary to achieve the greatest impact, it is appropriate to look at state and local levels for each category, and to look across jurisdictions. It will be necessary to involve multiple organizational levels within an agency. A primary objective is to build support and gain participation at the highest levels, at which incident management may currently have no visibility. This may also include key staff members of executives, whose influence on the agency's and therefore the program's direction can be considerable.

Stakeholders in the Milwaukee Traffic Incident Management Program

City of Brookfield, police and public works	Medical College of Wisconsin
City of Greenfield fire, police, public works	Northwestern University Traffic Institute
City of Milwaukee fire, police, public works, safety commission	Wisconsin Towing Association
	City of Glendale
Fond du Lac County sheriff	City of Menomonee Falls police
Ozaukee County highway commissioner and Sheriff	City of Wauwatosa fire and police
	City of West Allis fire, police, public works
Walworth County highway commissioner and sheriff	Kenosha County public works and sheriff
	Racine County public works and sheriff
Waukesha County highway commissioner and sheriff	Washington County highway commissioner and sheriff
Southeast Wisconsin regional planning commission	Illinois DOT and Toll Authority
	Wisconsin DOT
Wisconsin Department of Natural Resources	USDOT/FHWA
AAA Wisconsin	Interested consulting firms
Greater Milwaukee convention and visitors bureau	Marquette University
	Metro Networks
WTMJ Radio	Wisconsin Motor Carriers Association

There are also stakeholders who may be outside of the geographic area, such as the Federal Highway Administration division office and resource center, but who are interested and who can contribute in valuable ways. Similarly, it may be appropriate to involve, or at least inform, the headquarters components of such stakeholders as the state DOT or the state patrol even though they do not participate directly in incident management. Since most budget and personnel requests must be approved by these organizations, having their understanding and buy-in at upper levels will be valuable. These units also strongly influence statewide policy (such as on distribution of traveler information), which can impact the conduct of regional incident management.

Incident management is not necessarily easily understood by many of the stakeholders who have only peripheral involvement. Thus, it is critically important to understand how to explain incident management and communicate the importance effectively to these stakeholders. When working with the stakeholders, one key element in achieving success is to understand each stakeholder group's priorities, perspectives, and expectations for the incident management program. Often the overall organizational orientations differ. For example, the DOT may be focused on transportation efficiency and the state patrol on safety. The public and private sector motivations and timeframes may prove to be substantially different. Each stakeholder group will need to understand its role, how it will benefit, how its constituency will be served, and how it will be aided in carrying out its mission. As discussed earlier, perspectives may be different at different levels of a stakeholder organization, or may differ between different departments within an organization. Each group or level's perspective should be considered, and each should receive appropriate involvement and information.

Develop Program Goals and Objectives

Defining goals and a set of objectives for the program is critical. At the present time, few programs have documented goals and even fewer have documented objectives. The absence of clearly defined goals and corresponding objectives for the program can lead to difficulties in executing responsibilities during critical periods. Specifically, this situation can lead to misunderstandings among partners when they are faced with tough choices during budget cuts.

Goals and objectives must address needs. Therefore, those involved in developing the program must understand the relevant needs and problems, and how incident management can assist in resolving them. Such needs and problems will come both from the participating agencies (i.e., the law enforcement agency may be concerned about safety of officers at the incident scene) and from the regional perspective and broader than any single agency (i.e., there may be a general concern about the impact incident-related congestion is having on the region's economy).

The goals and objectives must be a coherent set representing those of the entire program and not merely a collection of goals and objectives from all of the stakeholders. Reconciling the differences between the partners and agreeing upon a set of common goals and objectives is absolutely critical for the program's success.

Implementing an Incident Management Program

In jointly developing the goals and objectives, it may be helpful to engage the stakeholders in a workshop environment. Using this approach:

- Will ensure that inputs are received from all key stakeholders and are well understood
- Will build a sense of ownership of the program
- May provide a forum in which preliminary issues can emerge and solutions can be developed.

To keep the discussion directed and to improve the likelihood that the workshop's objectives will be achieved, it may be beneficial to employ a trained facilitator who can organize the program, make arrangements for facilities and resources, and be responsible for recording and distributing the interactions that take place in the workshop.

As for any program, the goals and objectives should be clearly definable and performance measures should be developed which correspond to them. Goals and objectives should also be, to the extent possible, free of external influence, and of a nature such that the impact of external influences can be separated so that all benefits of the program are fully understood.

It is equally valuable to reflect the goals and objectives of the incident management program in each agency's higher level goals and objectives during the agency's periodic strategic planning process. The incident management program goals and objectives should also be tightly integrated with those expressed in the Regional Transportation Plan. Once in place, this linkage between the incident management program and the agency's and region's fundamental conceptual documents will support incorporation of incident management into mainstream activity.

**Goals and Objectives of Milwaukee's
Traffic Incident Management Program**

Goal 1. Improve and enhance freeway incident management, reducing the time to detect, verify, and clear traffic incidents

Goal 2. Improve freeway safety

    Objective 2.1   Reduce the number of traffic crashes

    Objective 2.2   Protect the emergency response personnel

    Objective 2.3   Improve response to hazardous materials incidents

    Objective 2.4   Reduce the response time of emergency medical services

    Objective 2.5   Educate drivers to improve their reaction to traffic incidents

Goal 3. Enhance the quality and efficiency of freeway travel

    Objective 3.1   Use existing freeway capacity to its fullest extent

    Objective 3.1   Provide more information to travelers

    Objective 3.2   Improve traffic management during traffic incidents

    Objective 3.3   Reduce vehicle emissions and improve air quality

Identify Institutional and Jurisdictional Challenges

In the process of coming to agreement on goals and objectives for the program, the institutional and jurisdictional differences emerge quickly. Identifying and recognizing these challenges will go a long way towards shaping a stable program. Organizing one or more workshops involving all stakeholders is a technique that can assist in developing the program goals and objectives quickly. It is best that these sessions be facilitated by individuals with no obvious allegiance to any of the stakeholders. Typically this could be someone from the federal government, the consulting community, or academia.

The following are examples of significant barriers that are identified when discussing goals and objectives. These barriers need to be overcome, as do issues that arise when implementing regional incident management programs.

- **Commitment of Resources**—The most serious institutional challenge affecting program development is commitment of resources, which come primarily from budgets approved by legislative bodies such as city councils, county councils, and state legislatures. Each legislative body has a corresponding chief executive (mayor, governor) who writes a budget for the agencies under his or her authority. The key to making an incident management program work is coordinating between agencies to assure that critical resources are available for the participating agencies. In a program, agencies support one another's requests for incident management resources, and assure that neither gaps nor overlaps exist.

- **Jurisdictional Issues/Barriers**—Jurisdictional issues surface when two or more agencies/organizations must respond to an incident but where their respective responsibilities are unclear, or if the immediate objectives of their field personnel conflict. Jurisdictional problem areas include definition of site responsibilities, field communications, legal ramifications, political sensitivity, perspectives of each agency, and administrative coordination among agencies. Jurisdictional barriers can require legislation, or may be overcome through executive level review and discussion or by examining and adapting roles in cross-jurisdictional situations.

- **Resource Constraints**—Sufficient resources (equipment, staff and funding) typically are not allocated specifically to incident management programs, which makes it difficult to sustain the programs over the long term. Most often, this situation occurs when incident management is considered as a lower tier priority of one or more participating organizations. The availability and allocation of resources both within and among agencies play significant roles in the selection and implementation of overall incident management strategies. Although resources are almost always limited for every partner, sharing of resources, alternate procurement approaches (leasing vs. buying), realistic planning, funding participation by more partners, identification of special funding, and privatization may offer relief from resource pressures.

- **Operational Procedures**—The multiple agencies who agree to allow their personnel to cooperate with partner agencies (even outside their traditional scope of operations) and to share equipment to respond to incidents need to develop and follow specific procedures that facilitate an appropriate and effective response to specific situations. Good communication among agencies at both the managerial and field levels, knowledge of the national Incident Command System used in natural disaster response, and understanding of the legal ramifications of specific operational decisions are key to optimizing operational procedures.

- **Training Needs**—In most cases, field personnel from one agency are not fully aware of the objectives and duties of their counterparts in cooperating agencies. Training of field personnel in their own incident management tasks must be complemented by an understanding of the duties and abilities of other agencies and the importance of cooperation among all agencies involved. Such an understanding of each others' duties and abilities, along with repeated interaction in planning, implementation, and analysis of incident responses, will build the trust necessary for rapid and well-coordinated response. Formal training of its own personnel by each agency is also an essential starting point. Joint training, simulations, and rehearsals can be highly effective approaches to improving interagency coordination, as well as after-action analyses.

- **Administrative Issues**—Administrative issues address the coordination and cooperation of the different divisions within each agency at the administrative level. Administrative problem areas include human resource management and internal turf battles over funding, staffing, equipment, and operations. Recruitment by multiple organizational units, identifying how each can support incident management once it is identified as an agency-wide initiative, involving less constrained third parties, and seeking win-win opportunities can assist in overcoming these problems.

- **Agency Commitment**—Incident management programs need to get buy-in from within the participating organizations themselves. This is true in particular for the law enforcement, fire, rescue, and other similar agencies that do not own the roadway infrastructure. These partners must be involved from the beginning, at multiple organizational levels all the way to the top, must understand their roles, and must have a clear vision of the reasons for the program and how their organizations will benefit. Formalization of the commitment—through memoranda of understanding, joint operating plans, or jointly signed strategic plans—is an ideal demonstration of that commitment. Participation of senior executives in an incident management steering committee not only regularly raises the awareness of these executives about incident management, but also provides each stakeholder with meaningful input to the strategic direction and major tactical decisions regarding how incident management is carried out.

- **Over-reliance on Technology**—Incident management programs are increasingly becoming technology-oriented and, broadly speaking, there is a push toward incorporating additional technology into operations. However, incident management technology, like Intelligent Transportation Systems, is nothing more than a tool for incident management personnel. Without the correct training and application, it can be a costly investment that will serve the needs of neither the public nor the service providers. Organizations must recognize that technology by itself will not solve the institutional issues that affect incident management.

- **Lack of Clear Leadership**—A champion for incident management is often required to coordinate and implement an interagency incident management program. This person, or group of persons, rallies organizations, each with its own missions and goals, around the incident management cause. Without a champion, it is more difficult to build support and sustain the momentum necessary to implement a program. The champion often serves as spokesperson (to multiple audiences) for the program, and leads efforts to build support and acquire or justify the resources that the program needs. The champion may also be a visionary, defining the program and providing a strategy and sense of direction for the program. The champion often provides continuity for the program as individual participants arrive and depart. The champion is also ideally a strong conduit for communication with agency executives and key staff and support departments, as well as with incident management leaders at other participating agencies.

Addressing institutional challenges is critical for the sustained success of any regional incident management program. Incident management programs that do not have a solid institutional foundation and which rely solely on the leadership of a single champion, or on temporary synergies created by interagency coordination for special events, may fall apart over the long term. The critical factor for the long-term success and sustainability of an incident management program is its institutionalization and multilevel commitment across all agencies involved. Thus, the development and implementation of strategies to overcome the institutional challenges previously mentioned is of utmost importance when organizing incident management programs.

Phase II: Program Development

The program development phase involves activities that will result in a comprehensive incident management program. The steps in Program Development are:

- Obtain buy-in from stakeholders
- Develop performance measures for objectives
- Develop an incident management program strategy and plan
- Implement the plan.

Obtain Buy-in from Stakeholders

Once the stakeholders are identified in the concept phase, they must formalize their commitment to the program. Many will already be participating in incident management activity through performance of their respective duties. Within these organizations, the appropriate key participants and decision makers must be convinced that formalizing the program will have meaningful benefits, and that it is consistent with their own best interests and those of their organizations. This is most often accomplished on a peer-to-peer basis within the agency or between the agencies, building on existing relationships, understanding, and trust created while managing incidents.

Implementing an Incident Management Program

The challenge of building buy-in is encountered both when dealing with other agencies, and when dealing with other departments within one's own agency/organization. Ensuring involvement of and acceptance by other participating units is equally critical, and requires the same identification of shared benefits and common goals as with partner agencies/organizations.

The process of formalizing buy-in starts with identifying and agreeing upon a basic set of program goals and objectives. As an incident management program grows in scope, new partners join in and new responsibilities are added. Obtaining stakeholders' buy-in is an ongoing process.

The degree of success experienced in securing adequate funding is influenced by the extent of buy-in by senior agency officials. Adequacy of funding is typically less of an issue when there is strong support from senior organizational leaders because the initiator of the program often can garner the resources necessary to implement the program. In addition, a leader with enough power and respect among his or her peers and subordinates can persuade parties that might normally resist change, thus overcoming some of the risks inherent in program startup.

Most often the realization of the need for institutionalizing incident management and efforts toward it originate with middle management levels of participating organizations. The easiest way to create support for new activities is to build on such existing support and trust. This most often comes from building on existing relationships. If, for example, the state DOT and the state patrol are already working together on improving work zone safety or have partnered to operate a service patrol, it would be much easier to build on these existing organizational and personal relationships and trust to support the incident management program, rather than to start with relationships that have no existing foundation.

Once one or more relationships are in place, the program concept is viewed as being more legitimate and realistic, and it is often easier to persuade less familiar partners to join the effort, and more senior officials to provide their support. Working through some of the fundamental issues using existing relationships where communication is more frank and forthright may also expose some of the more complex issues, and will allow preliminary approaches to be prepared or initial hurdles to be overcome.

Support of mid-level management and supervision within the partner agencies is an important component of building a high level of cohesion and morale at the working levels of the partners. Some of these managers develop into champions of the programs shortly after its commencement. Periodic meetings of personnel who carry out daily incident and traffic management activity can be equally beneficial, both in building understanding which leads to more effective practices, and in building trust and cooperation. A program that does not have the support of the supervisors and staff cannot live up to its full potential, even if funding and equipment are available to do the work. This is especially true in programs that are dependent on the good will of personnel from other agencies or divisions to staff a transportation management center or manage incident management efforts after hours.

In order to obtain support from all levels and stakeholders, lines of communication must be opened early in the process and increasing levels of trust must be established. Care must be taken to ensure that none of the stakeholders or their interests and contributions are taken for granted. It is advisable to set up a system to recognize individuals and organizations for obtaining stakeholder buy-in and fostering interagency cooperation. Interagency working groups are one way to accomplish this objective. A supplemental approach is to engage the stakeholders through extensive outreach that demonstrates the benefits of implementing an efficient incident management program to both the public at-large and the individual agencies and organizational levels involved. While success cannot be guaranteed just because all parties recognize the benefits of an incident management program, the widespread support that arises from the combined approach can help ensure that a program will be effective and sustainable in the long term.

Buy-in must occur across all levels of the partner organizations involved in the program. An integrated approach involving both supervisory/management levels and senior agency leadership is the best suited to obtain broad-based buy-in at all levels of the stakeholder organizations. Often the senior officials are less familiar with incident management, and may not be directly involved on a continual basis, even on a steering committee. In such cases, it is important that the participating individuals understand what is needed in order to persuade their superiors, and be armed with the right resources in order to do this successfully.

Develop Performance Measures for Objectives

Tracking progress of the program's performance through evaluations is critical to its long-term sustainability and continuous improvement. While technically part of the third implementation phase, the consideration of measures actually begins earlier when measures to track the program's progress are defined. For each objective developed in the concept phase, a set of measures should be identified to track performance against the objective. These measures must be jointly selected by all core stakeholders involved to ensure that the partners do not interpret the objectives differently; that there is commitment to collecting, analyzing, and acting upon the data; and that the chosen measures will assist all partners in demonstrating to key internal decision makers the value of their continued, active participation in the program.

The measures must have both local and national perspectives. They should represent local needs in order to be relevant to the stakeholders. They should also be consistent with successful practices from similar programs, thus avoiding some of the mistakes made by other programs.

Some objectives are apparent and can be both directly measured and easily related to positive benefits. Objectives such as reducing the number of secondary incidents or decreasing average incident duration are examples of these. Others will be more difficult to measure objectively and link to benefits to the public.

Implementing an Incident Management Program

There may be active objections to measuring performance against objectives. While lack of measures makes it difficult to justify or improve performance, this lack also makes it impossible to criticize declining performance. Further, there is often concern about spending money on collection of data which "could be better spent getting the job done". This objection is often voiced when one agency's assistance is needed to collect data which supports not its own information needs, but those of another agency.

For more detail on the process of developing performance measures, please refer to Appendix A.

Develop an Incident Management Program Strategy and Plan

The development of a documented strategy and plan to develop the program is the most critical and time-intensive step in this phase. In order to achieve the far reaching task of creating a formal incident management program, it is essential that the participants first understand and agree upon what they want to achieve and how they will undertake this effort. It is far too easy to simply continue incident management activity as it is currently being carried out, considering the strategy development and planning efforts to be an administrative exercise without merit. However, investing the effort to develop the strategy can help in many ways. The strategy can:

- Define and provide a sense of the extent of the needs and problems that are being addressed, and state what is presently being done to address them
- Outline a series of methods and approaches for formalizing the incident management program
- Identify program functions and components, clarifying the full range of stakeholders
- Outline an overall schedule, funding strategy, and leadership approach
- Provide a way of formally identifying and agreeing upon roles and responsibilities of each partner
- Allow identification of needs and commitment of resources
- Provide a clear vision so that each partner can formulate realistic expectations
- Provide guidance on what actions are needed to move the program forward, and a description of the destination toward which it is moving
- Identify risks that the program is likely to experience, and develop risk mitigation approaches that can be put in place
- Provide context for the program, relative to the primary objectives of each participant, and with respect to related types of activity
- Provide tools that can be shared with senior decision makers, participants, and outside parties (such as the legislature) to understand the program's purpose and methods.

The plan is a detailed blueprint for carrying out the strategy successfully and can include the following components:

- Design plan for each incident management component (e.g., service patrols, incident detection, etc.) with the partner agency or agencies that will develop them
- Procurement plan and budget for each component with the appointment of a specific partner as the procurement agency
- Program schedule with timelines and contingency measures
- Training program, with the need for specific training courses and related material clearly identified
- Public relations plan and internal agency awareness strategies
- A list of early successes and small steps forward such as service patrols and enhanced location reference marking
- Incorporation of incident management into the transportation planning process
  — Tying incident management into the transportation plans' primary goals and objectives
  — Incorporating incident management into both components of appropriate budget elements and into stand-alone line items where appropriate
- Detailed budget for every component of the program with identified sources for the amounts listed.

Developing a strategy and detailed plan involves support from all stakeholder agencies/organizations and levels, and requires skills in various facets of incident management, operations, cost estimating, management models, training, and risk management. No one partner agency/organization is likely to have all these skills and, even if these skills are available, their staff are often too busy to devote the required levels of attention to developing a good plan. It is best if the development of this strategy and plan is assigned to outside experts who work closely with the stakeholders involved. A steering committee composed of senior executives of the partner agencies could oversee the development of the strategy. The strategy would benefit from their input, reflecting the perspectives of the participants, and would have a high degree of commitment from senior organizational leadership. The development of the plan could be overseen by a program committee composed of mid-level and senior managers from the stakeholder agencies.

Sharing "best practices" information from locations with established incident management programs will be useful in developing a forward-looking strategy that takes advantage of previous successes and failures. Touring a few of these locations is useful for the program committee in order to make specific recommendations for the plan.

The development of the strategy and plan consumes varying lengths of time, depending on the size and scope of the program being developed. This plan should be developed in phases so that the earlier phases can commence while the plan is being finalized. A period of about a half year, with some activity commencing as early as three months, would be reasonable to complete the strategy and plan. Any longer, and stakeholders run the risk of too much planning and too little action, especially in the eyes of senior agency executives.

> **Maryland CHART Plans Provide Basis for Legislative Support**
>
> *Early in the CHART program's development, the MdSHA recognized the need for both strategic and tactical guiding documents. These documents provided the foundation for the CHART program, and served as an important tool for communication with the state's legislature. The plans are updated annually, reflecting the program's accomplishments and impact, its activities, and its plans for the next several years.*

The strategy and plan are not the only documents which will be required. Incident management programs should be "mainstreamed" into the traditional transportation planning process at an early stage. Properly integrating the program's budgetary and staffing needs into the transportation planning process will constitute a major step toward a more secure funding position for continuing operations, and towards the provision of access to the capital funds necessary over time. This will also make it easier to identify the linkage between overall highway operations and incident management, so actions necessitated by changes in the transportation network are more easily identified and accommodated.

Implement the Plan

The last activity in this phase is the implementation of the plan itself. This step must be uniquely tailored to suit the needs, funds, and other constraints of the program being developed, and to take advantage of activity already underway and relationships and agreements that already exist between participating organizations. These aspects should have been addressed during the plan development. Often, transition to a full, formal program fails due to poor planning or loss of funding. If the plan is developed to the satisfaction of the stakeholders and their respective key senior executives, and the assumptions are realistic, it is much more likely that the transition will be successful and on time.

It will be helpful to have an operations-oriented program committee representing the key stakeholders lead the effort. This committee will be able to closely monitor the program's progress and results, and will be able to act relatively quickly to redirect the efforts and keep the program on track.

Since multiple agencies will be involved in the procurement of systems, personnel, and other aspects of the program, the partner agencies may find it helpful to invest in program management services. If the incident management program also involves numerous ITS installations and systems integration, the need for a program manager becomes more critical as these components make implementation prone to long delays and losses in functionality. Such a program manager should be able to provide both manpower and scarce technical and management skills which can facilitate more rapid and smooth program progression.

The length of time for transition to a formalized incident management program could range anywhere from a few months to several years depending on the scope and complexity of the program's components. Generally, it is possible to begin a functioning incident management effort with several basic features within a half-year from the start of implementation.

Program growth and progression is an ongoing process in the sense that the plan undergoes revisions. Goals and objectives (and therefore strategy) are reviewed and revised, and new budgets are implemented annually. The program will continue to evolve throughout its lifetime, reflecting new needs, participants, technology, capabilities, political realities, and personalities. Once the program is fully formalized, several tests can be applied to determine if it has progressed from being primarily a series of activities occurring in parallel to being a fully cohesive incident management program:

- Is the program ongoing and institutionalized?
- Is there a documented program plan? For more details on developing a program plan, please refer to the Lessons Learned section.
- Is the program formalized, is it interjurisdictional, and does it have an interorganizational structure?
- Is the program cross-functional and multidisciplinary, supporting all primary partners as peers?
- Are there regular functions to facilitate communications and joint decision making?

A list of documents on the operation of incident management programs is presented in the References section of this document.

Phase III: Program Maintenance and Sustainability

Once an incident management program has begun, keeping it operating and growing presents an additional set of challenges. Addressing these challenges requires carrying forward the activities started during the Program Concept phase. Continuing operation also requires an understanding of how well the program is performing, and then modifying the direction which was initially developed in order to ensure that the program most effectively provides the benefits identified in the initial goals/objectives process.

The steps in Program Maintenance and Sustainability are:

- Solidify relationships with stakeholders
- Evaluate performance against every objective

Implementing an Incident Management Program

- Modify strategy and plan based on evaluation
- Leverage public support
- Use the transportation planning process to secure funding in the long term.

This third phase focuses on maintaining and sustaining the program. These activities do not occur without deliberate effort, and are easily neglected when the program's leadership is heavily involved in day-to-day operations. Incident management goals, objectives, and activities must be consistent with the overall role of each agency since traffic incident management activities may be viewed as being secondary to the overall goals of specific agencies. Without attention and if not viewed as a critical component of the participating agencies' missions, the incident management effort can find itself in a very vulnerable position when the annual funding cycle arrives, or when new resources are needed in order to expand the mission or coverage area.

Incident management programs are highly dependent on operations funding from their participating agencies. For traditionally construction-oriented transportation departments and departments of public works, this form of funding is often the most scarce. Historically, operations funding has had a greater dependence on the state/local revenue base rather than the extensive leverage received from federal matching funds. Public safety and emergency services agencies face the reverse situation: their historical operations focus means that their budgets are predominantly operations funding. Such agencies may have significant difficulty in obtaining meaningful blocks of funding for capital items, such as for interfaces between their radio systems and those of partner agencies, to support the improved incident management program. In most agencies, until incident management is viewed as a mainstream agency activity area, it automatically has a lower priority for either new or continuing funding.

A formal incident management program must address what can be done to position itself to compete effectively for scarce funds from each partner organization. Primary benefits of formalizing the program include providing documentation of the need and the program's vision for the legislative budget-making process, and raising the program's visibility and stature to key executives.

Program sustainability also refers to the program's ability to weather a difficult evolutionary path. Events such as loss of a program champion or a change in administration can threaten the program's existence, and therefore deserve consideration in planning and preparation.

Solidify Relationships with Stakeholders

Relationships among stakeholders must never be taken for granted, even though they might appear rock solid. Every possible effort must be made to continuously strengthen these relationships even when it appears that things are just fine. As with the earlier activity in building the relationships, it is important to identify all appropriate departments and levels within the stakeholder organizations, and to solidify relationships throughout the levels and departments which are necessary to carry the incident management program forward.

Solidifying the relationships will often combine two important elements: constant and effective communication, and a message that will build continued support. Constant and effective communication is often as simple as making sure that stakeholders are informed of progress and successes, and are involved in addressing issues and opportunities. Incident management programs, particularly those that do not have major physical assets such as a transportation management center, may be achieving very positive results, but with little visibility. Thus, stakeholders may be unaware of the program's activity until it is highlighted in the media (unfortunately seldom in a positive light) or until the annual budgetary cycle arrives. It is not beneficial to have stakeholders questioning the value of the program, or their importance to it during such times. Actively involving the stakeholders in the program, perhaps through regular meetings and especially in program improvement activities such as "after-action analyses," will make them feel that they are an important part of a valuable program, and that they can exert meaningful influence over its course. Periodic updating of the incident management strategy is an excellent opportunity to solicit input from senior executives, and to ask for their review and approval of the program's direction.

Even when the program has a name recognized separately from the stakeholder agencies (such as Maryland's CHART or Milwaukee's Traffic Incident Management Enhancement [TIME] program), it can be beneficial to recognize the key participating entities. This is a particularly important component when some portion of the program, such as the service patrol or the traveler information program, is privatized. Continuing to show key agency and organization logos on the visible assets builds public support and provides recognition of the stakeholders' important contributions.

As with the development of relationships, sustaining relationships may also call for identifying ways that the partner organizations can support one another. These are most commonly found in situations where agencies can assist one another by jointly funding, procuring, or managing either staff or physical assets. A situation where one partner agency funds the service patrol vehicles, but another provides the personnel to dispatch and staff them or the fuel, maintenance, and other resources to keep them operating, can be a powerful component of the partnership in which each partner benefits from the resources of the other(s).

Just as it was important while developing the goals and objectives, there may be a benefit to periodically bringing stakeholders together in a retreat-type forum to gather inputs, compare experiences, identify and address emerging issues, and discuss performance to date and the direction in which the program is headed.

Implementing an Incident Management Program

> **Bringing Together the Key Stakeholders**
>
> *Maryland's CHART program's board is chaired by the Maryland DOT's Chief Engineer, and includes as voting members district engineers from all CHART districts, the director of the Office of Traffic, the director of the Office of Maintenance, key contractors, and the Maryland Transportation Authority. All other interested agencies are also welcome to participate.*
>
> *Milwaukee's Freeway Incident Management Team and steering committee meetings include both large group and subgroup meetings (corridor incident management, freeway, special events management and outreach/awareness). Priorities for the Team are identifying issues, developing solutions, and coordinating deployment of solutions.*

> **Evaluation of Seattle's Incident Management Program**
>
> *One of the most studied programs in the country is located in Seattle, Washington. It was there that the Washington State Transportation Center (TRAC) teamed up with the Washington State Department of Transportation (WSDOT) to develop a series of evaluation documents on the regional incident management programs in Washington State, paying particular attention to the program in Seattle.*
>
> *These documents included pre-program studies regarding the costs and impacts of establishing an incident management program, program evaluations of incident response teams, and case studies. These documents have proven to be extremely useful in the evaluation and ongoing improvement of the Washington program's response and clearance times and even have been used as a tool for generating additional financing for service patrols and other program components.*

Evaluate Performance Against Every Objective

Tracking the program's performance against each objective identified in the concept phase is the only way to document changes in the overall program's performance. This is a critical need in light of continued budget shrinkage at most public sector concerns. Conducting a detailed evaluation of the program will allow managers to present program accomplishments as justification for continued funding.

There are important considerations to focus on while conducting a program evaluation. First, it has to be an objective and independent evaluation carried out by a reputable organization that is not part of the program itself. Engaging the services of an independent evaluator increases the credibility of the findings in the eyes of stakeholders, politicians, and the traveling public. Second, it is important to swiftly implement recommendations from any evaluation to alter the program's operation or future implementation plans (for scope expansion) based on the evaluation's findings. Since the evaluation is linked directly to program goals and objectives, the evaluation findings should provide a clear indicator of whether the program is satisfying the needs that brought it into being. Thus, modifications based on the findings should help steer the program toward better satisfying the identified needs.

For a more extensive description of the evaluation process, please refer to Appendix A.

Modify Strategy and Plan Based on Evaluation

The program's strategy may need to be modified periodically to address the new challenges the program is likely to encounter. Even though extensive planning is performed, difficulties which have not been anticipated and risks whose full impact was not foreseen in developing the risk mitigation plan may be encountered. Most of these are institutional in nature.

The most common changes in strategy (with possible methodologies to counter them) include:

- Working with a smaller budget, or with fewer or less-skilled personnel
  - Perhaps by using less overtime, leasing rather than buying, privatizing, using part-time staff, reducing coverage to priority corridors, or spreading the cost across more partners
- Growing more slowly than had been planned
  - Focusing on the most critical corridors, trading off capital for operating expenses, combining some functions with those performed by existing staff, or reducing the number of functions performed or the hours of operation
- Changes in roles and responsibilities among the program participants, and possibly withdrawal of participation or support by one or more participants
  - Identifying alternate service providers, or seeking a more equitable or acceptable balance of responsibilities
- Working with legal limitations on the types of activity the program can perform
  - Considering the need for legislation to remove such barriers, or perhaps trading roles
- Complications in working across jurisdictional boundaries
  - Identifying opportunities to provide benefits or to share resources with partners across jurisdictional lines, or seeking special funding for cross-border integration
- Being tasked with greater responsibility than had been anticipated (more functions, a more complex event such as the Olympic Games, or a larger geographic area of coverage)
  - Clearly understanding and documenting the requirements, identifying

Implementing an Incident Management Program

　　　　potential additional sources of and methods of obtaining funding and other resources, and participating in planning for such eventualities

- Being forced to regularly justify the existence of the program, explain the program's performance in an unusually difficult situation, or attempt to meet unrealistic expectations
  — Planning and implementing a thorough evaluation program, focused both on how the program can improve and on the measures that are important to key decision makers; also implementing regular and effective communication with the media and with decision makers at appropriate levels.

The best preparation for such eventualities is a combination of:

- Formalization of the program through various steps already described
- "Unification" of the program's budget across the multiple participating agencies
- Raising program visibility and stature
- Linking the program to the primary activity areas of each participating agency, or succeeding in having it promoted to being viewed as one of these primary activity areas
- Extensive and regular stakeholder involvement in program activity and evolution
- Program evaluation and outreach
- Continuing awareness of other programs in order to learn from their experiences
- Participation in incident management forums—such as the Institute for Transportation Engineers (ITE) Traffic Incident Management Committee, or the Institute of Electrical and Electronics Engineers Incident Management Working Group P1512—in order to learn about the latest technologies and management best practices
- Regular revisiting of the program's strategy.

This last activity provides the opportunity to examine the assumptions and conditions under which the program has been operating, as well as its actual performance. Through such self examination, program managers can have solutions in place as difficulties arise, rather than being forced into a reactive mode of response. The strategy update should be conducted at the same interval as the budget process (e.g., annually or biennially), but well in advance of the budget submission. This schedule coordination supports timely movement on and mutual support of requests for additional resources within the partner agencies' appropriations cycles or legislative sessions. The strategy update will also provide the opportunity to examine (and, if appropriate, revise) the existing goals and objectives, providing more realistic measures of program performance, and perhaps setting better standards which the program can seek to attain. Performance on those measures can also be assessed at this point (and likely more often), and decisions made on what actions may be needed in order to achieve desired levels of effectiveness.

The strategy update should periodically include a close look at the goals and objectives which drive the program. As the program makes progress, objectives will be achieved and new objectives will emerge. Other objectives may become irrelevant as time passes and conditions change. Technological evolution may also cause a need to make changes in the direction of the program. This review will help ensure that the program continues to address the issues which its partners face.

Leverage Public Support

It is important to communicate the benefits of the program to the stakeholders and the public at large. This communication will help maintain the high levels of support necessary to protect the program against budget cuts, and foster improved relationships among the partner agencies.

The plan should contain a public relations component which addresses maintaining support. The plan should consider the audiences which need to be reached and the various methods of communication available to the agency. This will likely combine regular efforts by the agency and taking advantage of fortuitous occasions. For internal distribution, agency newsletters may be an effective start with little cost. Critical to external relations is developing a strong outreach and training program designed to incorporate several agencies, the private sector, and the media.

The best programs across the country leverage good publicity. Successful programs also take advantage of special events in their own operations by involving key program supporters. Even small activities, such as "christening the fleet" of new service patrol vehicles or ribbon cutting at the new TMC control room, provide opportunities to make the senior executives feel a sense of ownership. The executives, in turn, can demonstrate their support of the program's positive outcomes within the stakeholder organizations and to the public.

Use the Transportation Planning Process to Secure Funding in the Long Term.

While many operational staff find the traditional transportation planning process to be overly bureaucratic and cumbersome, the benefits of developing plan elements that support incident management and integrating these into the transportation planning process far outweigh the negatives. It is through avenues such as these that Intelligent Transportation Systems grew at such a phenomenal rate, raising technology to the line-item level in both state and national budgets. With the passage of legislation, such as the Intermodal Surface Transportation and Efficiency Act (ISTEA) in 1991 and the Transportation Equity Act for the 21st Century (TEA-21) in 1998, opportunities abound to secure additional funding for incident management program activities. These opportunities should not be ignored. It is necessary to have major projects included in the Transportation Improvement Plan (TIP) or Statewide Transportation Improvement Plan (STIP).

Implementing an Incident Management Program

> **Outreach From TransGuide Takes Many Forms**
>
> *Outreach for some incident management programs has grown to include full-time staff and/or dedicated contractor resources. The TransGuide program began accessing services from the Texas DOT's public affairs office over a year before it went into operation. By the date of operation, it had a full-time communications staff member assigned, with an office in the transportation management center. That person's efforts were supplemented by an outreach component in the TransGuide implementation contract, which provided the program with roadside signs, a logo, literature, videos, and display materials. The program and implementation contractor staff dedicated many hours to speaking to community groups, ranging from school groups to fraternal organizations. The communications person also built on existing agency relationships with the media, and built new ones. Program staff were regularly interviewed, and even spoke on radio talk shows. As the program implementation culminated in the system's official opening, the local morning newspaper ran a two-week series of editorial cartoons supporting the program!*

Several successful programs are now seeking to separate both their incident management operations and budget process from other divisions within the same organization. The expectation is that the long-term benefits of securing funding on an annual or biennial basis specifically for incident management programs and services will help institutionalize the program at the organizational level and reduce the risk of cutbacks or elimination.

Components of the Transportation Planning Process

Transportation Planning Activities
There is a broad array of activities that ultimately result in a set of recommended, fundable transportation projects and programs. These activities feed information to the principal products of the transportation planning process: the transportation plan and TIP. The process varies from one area to another and includes input from many agencies and individuals. These transportation planning activities include policy definition, corridor/sub-area studies, strategic assessments, etc.

Transportation Plan
The plan is a primary product of the planning process. It is prepared periodically by each state and metropolitan area. The plan documents the policy direction for the region and describes how transportation projects and programs will be implemented over a 20-year (or longer) period. It has sometimes been called the long-range plan, but it includes the entire time period out to the horizon year, including both short-range and long-range projects and programs. Projects for ITS need to be included in this document.

Transportation Improvement Plan
A document that must be prepared periodically by each state and metropolitan area that describes specific projects to be constructed and/or operated over the next several years (minimum three years; some areas include additional years).

Implementation
The actual implementation of the transportation plan design, construction, and operation of the projects included in the TIP.

Performance Evaluation
Evaluation of the results achieved from the implementation of the TIP, assessing its effectiveness and making adjustments as necessary to both the transportation plan and the TIP.

(Integrating Intelligent Transportation Systems Within the Planning Process: An Interim Handbook, FHWA, 1998)

Implementing an Incident Management Program

> **CHART's Approach to Developing Sustainable Relationships Through Mutual Support**
>
> *When Maryland's CHART program was starting up, it was a challenge to establish the relationships necessary between the participating agencies—Maryland State Highway Administration, Maryland State Police (MSP), and Maryland Transportation Authority (MdTA). As the nucleus agency, MdSHA found it useful to build relationships with other key agencies by cooperatively funding joint needs.*
>
> *For example, MdSHA agreed to fund several necessary items for MSP, including paint for outlining crash scenes, facilities improvements for the jointly-staffed traffic operations centers, and fully equipped motorcycles that could be used for reaching crash scenes during peak travel hours. In return, MSP has collocated full-time staff at the statewide operations center (SOC).*
>
> *Based on this success, CHART has extended the approach to outside organizations, including the media. Agreements were developed that allow local radio and television stations to be patched into live closed-circuit television feeds from the SOC. In exchange, traffic helicopters owned and operated by local stations provide real-time views of traffic incidents and delays to CHART. Radio broadcasts are also shared between the organizations.*

Regional Traffic Incident Management Programs

Part 6: Lessons Learned in Implementing and Sustaining Incident Management Programs

Take advantage of attention focused on major events (international games, weather events, earthquakes, etc.) to help organize and build support for a formal incident management program.

While some of these events cannot be anticipated, it is important to set the stage for success. Begin organizing interagency working groups and building the case for a program *prior* to a major event or crisis. Then, once an event occurs, take advantage of the media attention and public outcry to focus attention and resources on organizing a coordinated incident management program. In other words, *strike while the iron is hot!*

**Taking Advantage of an Opportunity:
Georgia DOT and the Atlanta Olympics**

"You cannot wait for a crisis or international event to occur before organizing incident management agencies. Start the program and dialogue prior to any event, and the event will help solidify those relationships."—Steve Parks, Deputy Commissioner, Georgia Department of Transportation (GDOT).

In the 1970s the GDOT Commissioner tried and failed to organize an interagency incident management program. It wasn't until 1992 that the Chief of Georgia's Emergency Management Agency (GEMA) began to include law enforcement and GDOT in emergency response.

However, it was the announcement that Atlanta would host the 1996 Summer Olympics that was the real catalyst for mobilization. The GDOT Director of Operations helped organize the program because of his experience and his relationships within his agency.

Critical to the success of this effort was the identification of a "credible nucleus" that recognized that many agencies had a role in managing incidents. In Georgia, this was GEMA.

While it is important to understand that agencies cannot be forced to work together, if a viable framework is in place, a major event can help mobilize and solidify support for a coordinated interagency program.

Obtain and leverage political support when it is available.

Since transportation funding is often politically influenced and transportation policy is an important item on political agendas, support of political leaders for transportation projects is essential. Obtaining political support is particularly important for incident management programs since they do not offer publicity-

Lessons Learned in Implementing and Sustaining Incident Management Programs

laden opportunities such as ribbon-cutting ceremonies for new roads or bridges. Obtaining political support is an important step for the success and sustainability of any incident management program. This step requires informing leaders about the benefits of incident management and convincing them of the need for a formal program. It also can be accomplished by taking advantage of scenarios such as the one in Houston.

> **Houston's Mayor Catalyzes Incident Management and the TranStar ITS Center**
>
> *Mayor Lanier of Houston encountered severe traffic congestion on the way to a Houston Oilers football game. He called his staff several times, but no one could give him accurate information about what was happening or how long the congestion might last. He reached the game close to half-time. The next day he initiated action to ensure that his experience would not be repeated by Houston area citizens.*
>
> *Thus, the Houston area's first incident management program and the Houston TranStar ITS system were born. The mayor, a previous member of the State Transportation Board, led an effort to gain the cooperation of the other agencies in the Houston area. His efforts enabled TxDOT, Houston METRO, and the Houston Police Department to gain top management buy-in for their portions of the incident management program. The result was an incident management program developed in a very short time. A new mayor is in office now, but the programs still thrives, despite the loss of its initial champion.*

Ongoing successes are important.

The program will need to have some ongoing, visible successes in order to sustain interest by participants and to keep the funding flowing. It is important to realize, however, that the full scope of benefits may not be immediately visible or easily measured. Because of this, effort must be focused on keeping the program moving forward and on identifying successes. Successes can sometimes be derived from special circumstances, such as a service patrol providing aid and comfort to a school bus full of stranded youngsters[5]. If there are no visible winners, it will be difficult for some major participants to remain involved.

The program needs involvement from the right organizational levels.

Key program committees will need to have someone attend from each key stakeholder group who has adequate authority to speak for his/her organization. These representatives should also have the ear of the senior executives at their organizations. It is important to also involve middle and working level people in the organizations who can serve as organizational champions for incident

---

[5] Improving Mobility Saving Lives Safety Service Patrols, USDOT, 1999

management. It can be fatal to depend exclusively on the participation of very senior people, as they will often not have the time to meet on a regular basis.

Procedures should not threaten the agencies' own roles.

A sure way to alienate a key partner is to say that its involvement in incident management will change its responsibilities at the incident scene. The key to effective incident management is not shifting roles, but working together effectively in a coordinated manner, and perhaps taking slightly different actions which consider a broader set of goals than those of any single agency. Each partner will continue to be held accountable (by its senior management, other units of government, and the public) for its role in managing the incident, and for addressing those components of an incident (public safety, safety of involved personnel, safety of incident victims, environment, traffic flow) with which it is charged. Incident management should allow each partner to perform its duty, but with consideration for the duties of others and in coordination with them.

Identify realistic goals and make sure that expectations are met.

Formulating goals is always an exercise in balance. The goals must be aggressive enough that they will foster enthusiasm, but not so aggressive as to be unrealistic. They should create realizable expectations, whose achievement can be measured and communicated. The risk of setting goals too high is that the program may be perceived as a failure. Goals that cannot be measured may be viewed as a sign that the participants have no confidence in the program. Goals that are set too low may not be viewed as demonstrating a true value for the community or justifying the investment. In each case, the interest will wane, and participants are likely to withdraw their support.

Make the interagency incident management program a "win-win" for all stakeholders involved.

Stakeholders must perceive that there is a benefit to changing the *status quo*. Most organizations already perform some level of incident management and may not see the potential benefits in working in a structured, coordinated fashion with other agencies that do not share a common goal.

The first step in gaining buy-in from all stakeholders is to develop a common program goal that recognizes the different priorities among agencies. For example, DOTs may be more interested in the safe and efficient restoration of traffic flow, while fire departments may focus more on the individual safety of their personnel while clearing an incident. This difference of interests can create institutional and physical bottlenecks when the two organizations try working together to clear an incident from the roadway. By working together in an atmosphere of mutual respect and trust, several regions have been able to come to new agreements about how to meet each agency's goals while working toward a common goal of public safety and service.

Lessons Learned in Implementing and Sustaining Incident Management Programs

Resolve internal conflicts first.

Prior to working with outside agencies to develop a program, organizations must look inside their own walls to resolve potential conflicts between departments. Often, new programs create divides with regard to funding and chain of command that can jeopardize the success of a program. Sometimes a strong leader with enough power to force organizational change is enough to ensure implementation and sustainability. More often than not, however, program leaders come from mid- and lower-level management and must build a credible incident management effort before senior executives will endorse incident management and consistently promote it as an agency priority. Once internal implementation challenges have been overcome, agencies involved in incident management can focus on developing their external relationships with one another, as well as with the private sector, elected officials, and the public at-large. There are several options for developing long-term sustainable external relations. Good public relations are key to raising public awareness for a product or service which will ensure funding year after year.

Overcoming Internal Challenges: Implementation in WSDOT

The Washington State Department of Transportation piloted its modest but highly successful service patrol under the leadership of its Engineering division, but decided to develop its full incident management program under its Maintenance division. Placing the program under Maintenance was complicated by Maintenance staff's perception that an engineer had forced the implementation of an unnecessary program. Eventually, incident management was assigned to Traffic Operations, and funded as a separate line item in the Traffic Operations budget.

An individual from the Maintenance division was later named to head Seattle's Incident Management program. The combination of removing Incident Management from Maintenance and hiring a Maintenance person to lead the program has alleviated many of the problems that existed in the program's early years.

Sharing resources to overcome shortfalls can help build and solidify relationships among organizations.

When just starting off, agencies should look at how scarce resources can be shared to help distribute the burden of implementing a new program. As in the CHART example earlier, the DOT may be able to purchase for the law enforcement agency special equipment which speeds crash scene response. Oftentimes, benefits beyond the incident management program can be identified from such an agreement. This practice can continue to yield benefits as a regular practice as the incident management program grows and matures; it is not limited to the program's early phases.

Create dependencies to ensure program sustainability.

Developing a clear 'dependency' on the program and its offerings is one way to ensure its visibility and stability for the long term. Public leaders and travelers come to expect the services and improved conditions that result from the program. Thus, it becomes part of the budget baseline, rather than an optional item. The Atlanta case clearly illustrates success of this approach. Other locations have also employed this approach with success.

Atlanta's Highly Popular HERO Service Patrol

Sustaining interest and support (both financial and popular) is one of the toughest challenges any incident management program faces after its initial success. Atlanta has isolated its HEROs (Highway Emergency Response Operators) freeway service patrol from political and financial vulnerabilities by cultivating dependency on its services.

The HEROs are a highly visible arm of the incident management program. GDOT is deluged with letters of appreciation for their service. "Our public and our partners could not imagine living without our HEROs", says Marion Waters of GDOT. "They are dependent on them on a daily basis." The positive responses and publicity that the Atlanta program receives puts the pressure on politicians and policymakers to sustain and grow the program. This provides the best protection from any threats to the entire incident management program, even the less visible operations that are most vulnerable to budget cuts.

Prepare for the possibility that a leader might leave.

Successful leaders are difficult to retain in any organization, and particularly difficult to retain in the public sector. Often they are promoted internally or hired away by the private sector, leaving a leadership "vacuum" if no one has been designated as a successor. This lack of clearly-defined leadership following loss of a successful champion can cause incident management to lose momentum, sometimes causing the eventual breakdown of interagency relationships which had been established at a person-to-person level.

> *Future leaders should be chosen not simply for their management experience, but because they exhibit qualities that would allow them to build and sustain an interagency team of incident management professionals.*

Overcoming the loss of a champion requires the consideration of a leadership succession model. This model should consist of the identification and preparation of one or more additional persons who participate in the incident management program who can be prepared to assume leadership responsibilities should the current champion leave. Such preparation will likely be informal and performed within the incident management program, rather than part of an individual's career development program within his or her home agency. Ideally, each agency will see its incident management focal point as a key individual, and will take steps to ensure that a successor is identified and prepared in advance of such a departure.

Critical to the success of this model is its *early* implementation. If there is no effort to begin preparing a qualified, capable, and recognized successor until the current leader gives notice, it is unlikely that the new leader will have the understanding necessary to succeed.

Coordinate across jurisdictions/regions for technology and infrastructure planning.

By coordinating technology and infrastructure plans regionally rather than locally, benefits related to interoperability of technology and infrastructure management can be addressed prior to implementation, helping to reduce future costs and delays. This technique is often employed for ITS, but too frequently neglected by incident management leaders. Several regional programs exist in the United States that employ the regional planning method, including the Gary-Chicago-Milwaukee Corridor and the I-95 Corridor Coalition.

Commit to administrative support of an ongoing interorganizational structure and communication and decision-making events and meetings.

Any undertaking as complex as an incident management program requires some level of administrative support, and a regular forum (or forums) at which performance is reviewed, issues are raised, information is shared, and program change and evolution are discussed and approved. An incident management program will require this type of support and activity in order to function effectively. It is important, however, to arrive at a level of activity acceptable to all partners, some of whom may have difficulty justifying extended absences from the workplace to attend meetings. This is particularly true if the program has a steering committee composed of senior executives from participating organizations. Obtaining a significant commitment of time from such officials is often difficult or impossible. A much better plan is to ask for a realistic time commitment and to carry out a larger portion of the work in subordinate committees.

Part 7: Conclusion

The traffic impact of incidents on the nation's roadways is a major drain on productivity, causes increased stress to motorists, harms air quality, and is often the source of additional incidents. The nature of the incident scene presents numerous hazards to those involved in incidents and to those responding to the incident. Planned, organized regional incident management programs offer the promise of minimizing these negative consequences. Transforming incident management from simply a series of parallel activities into a formal, organized, coordinated, and well-documented program—and sustaining such programs—is a complex process, often involving a variety of organizations and multiple units and levels within some organizations. The differences in focus and approach by the different organizations requires that this joint undertaking be planned, implemented, and operated in a highly coordinated manner, with ongoing, effective communication at many organizational levels. This communication, as well as a thorough understanding of each agency's procedures and motivations, cultivates trusting relationships between involved individuals. Formalizing the program is essential to its success, but is much more easily done wrong than right, with possibly highly negative effects.

This document has presented a framework for organizing, implementing, and sustaining a regional incident management program. It has provided a step-by-step process broken into three phases, which should assist agencies in transitioning from existing incident management efforts to a formal incident management program. Although the framework is divided into discrete steps, it is much more likely that readers who implement these steps will experience a program that:

- Has a starting point with some elements already accomplished or in process
- Will evolve gradually rather than experience major demarcations between steps
- Will experience periods with several steps in process, as well as those with gaps in time between one step and the next.

The focus is institutional, rather than technical, and is based on:
- Understanding needs
- Defining the program
- Building and maintaining support
- Assessing the program's effectiveness
- Revising its approach to better address the needs.

The document has also provided lessons from the practical experiences of major incident management around the country. Through these experiences, it is hoped that new programs, or those undergoing stress and change, can avoid some of the challenges faced by early implementers, or can find the basis of workable solutions from the actions of those implementers.

Conclusion

The document's appendix provides more detail on two important steps: developing a strategy, and evaluating results.

Based on experiences from around the country, incident management programs can have a clear, positive effect. Particularly in areas suffering from significant recurrent congestion, incident management is a tool which can have highly visible positive results, generating public support and laudable benefit/cost ratios (such as Maryland's 5.6:1). Such programs deserve consideration, and it is hoped that this document, and its companion brochures, cross-cutting study, and handbook will be of value to organizations ready to begin their own incident management program.

Appendix A: Incident Management Monitoring, Evaluation, and Reporting of Benefits/Influence

Continual monitoring and evaluation are critical to the sustained success of any incident management program. Based on the findings of the evaluation, changes to strategic plans should be made. This continual improvement will result in a dynamic program that meets the public's changing needs. It is important that the evaluation be both independent and objective. Many times an outside vendor, such as a consulting firm or university, can perform a thorough and authoritative evaluation within a reasonable time period at a competitive rate.

At a minimum, assessments should be performed on response and clearance times over a period of a year or more. A thorough cost/benefit analysis on technology, equipment, and services should also be included as part of a comprehensive evaluation. This information is essential to developing a viable business plan that can be submitted as part of the transportation planning process.

A typical evaluation of an incident management program should include, at a minimum, the following steps and components:

- **Develop Evaluation Goals and Measurable Objectives**

    For the evaluation to be useful, the qualities to be measured must relate to the program's goals and objectives. Further, they must be measurable, so that the evaluation represents facts, rather than the evaluator's subjective opinion. The following example illustrates the process of breaking down each evaluation goal into its component objectives, and then beginning consideration of where the necessary data may be obtained.

    Figure A-1: Sample Evaluation Goals and Objectives Table

Goal	Objective	Source
1.1 Assess the effectiveness of the incident management program in terms of decreasing traffic and increasing safety.	1.1.1 Compare pre- and post-program response and clearance times.	DOT Safety Patrols
	1.1.2 Compare the number of pre- and post-program secondary incidents.	DOT State Police

Appendix A

- **Collect Data**

    Once the evaluators identify the source of information to measure each objective, they have a number of tools at their disposal to collect the data. Tools may include using written surveys, making a phone call to the head of a division, holding a meeting with operational managers, or looking at the computer logs from TMC systems.

    The means of collecting data are critical, and only appropriate tools (such as the partial interview guide below) should be used. For example, it may not be prudent to send a written survey to the commissioner of a department of transportation. However, if the evaluators keep their audience in mind, identify the right information and sources, and are flexible and persistent when gathering information, data collection can run smoothly and efficiently.

    Figure A-2: Sample Questionnaire

    A. Incident Notification

    1. Who do you notify when you learn of an incident?
    2. How are they notified?
    3. In what order are notifications made?
    4. What information is provided to each recipient?
    5. How many get the same information?
    6. How often are updates made to the notification?
    7. How often do you receive requests for additional or updated information?
    8. How often do you receive requests for information from parties who are not ordinarily notified?

- **Analyze Data**

    Once a sufficient amount of information is gathered according to the criteria established in the evaluation goals and objectives table, evaluators should begin analyzing the data to verify the outcome of the identified evaluation goals.

Figure A-3: Sample Table for Analysis of Data

Objective	Analysis of Data	Conclusion
1.1.1 Compare pre- and post-program response and clearance times.	Response times decreased by 30 percent. Clearance times decreased by 20 percent.	Program had positive impact on response and clearance times.
1.1.2 Compare the number of pre- and post-program secondary incidents.	Secondary incidents decreased by 42 percent.	Incident management program (especially shortened response and clearance times) contributed to the significant drop in secondary incidents.

- **Develop Report**

    Several interim reports to program stakeholders may be required but, in the end, one final report should be developed that documents the incident management program goals, the evaluation strategy, and the outcome of the evaluation.

- **Make Recommendations**

    Recommendations may be included as part of the final report or be presented as a separate document. Recommendations should be prioritized according to areas of greatest need and ranked according to their feasibility. A recommendation that cannot be implemented because of seemingly insurmountable obstacles should not be included as part of a final report unless it includes a strategy for overcoming these obstacles.

    In the same vein, a timeline for implementing the recommendations should be included for illustrative purposes so that sequencing and dependencies are obvious to the audience.

Figure A-4: Sample Implementation of Recommendations Timeline

J	F	M	A	M	J	J	A	S	O	N
ADD 12 VEHICLES TO SAFETY PATROLS: EXPAND PATROLS										
	DEVELOP INVENTORY OF RESOURCES AT ALL PARTNER AGENCIES									
		TRAIN 160 NEW STATE POLICE OFFICERS					PRESENTATIONS AT 46 FIRE COMPANIES			
COMMENCE MONTHLY INCIDENT MANAGEMENT NEEDS & BENEFITS BRIEFINGS TO STATE LEGISLATORS & OTHER ELECTED OFFICIALS										

Acknowledgments

The report authors would like to thank all the people and organizations that contributed to this study, many of whom provided their time and guidance to make this effort a success.

In Maryland, we would like to extend our gratitude to the CHART program staff, including Alvin Marquess, Dale Lineweaver, and Dan Hering.

We would also like to thank the staff at the Georgia DOT, especially Deputy Commissioner Steve Parks, Marion Waters, and Joe Stapleton.

In Seattle, Sergeant Leslie Young of the State Police, Jerry Althauser, Bill Legg at TRAC, Roger Steinert, and David Berg allowed us to interrupt their busy work days at WSDOT.

In Milwaukee, Les Fafard, John Corbin, and Steve Young of the Wisconsin DOT, Inspector Stacey Black of the Milwaukee County Sheriff's Department, and Deputy Commander Patti Hansen of the Wisconsin State Patrol were extremely helpful.

Captain Tim Kelly and Felix Vara of Houston METRO provided insights on the Houston Incident Management Program. We also would like to thank Doug Wiersig of the City of Houston, Ric Sadler of Harris County, Chief Tom Lambert of Houston METRO, and Jannete Rash of the Towers Association for spending time with us to share their views.

Finally, we would like to acknowledge the warm response we received from the Institute of Electrical and Electronics Engineers, (IEEE) Traffic Incident Management Working Group in developing the scope and content of this document. Many of its members contributed practical insight that shaped the look and feel of this document.

References

Colorado DOT, Business Plan & Marketing Strategy, 1996

FHWA, Assessment of ITS Deployment: Review of Metropolitan Areas, Discussions of Crosscutting Issues, 1996

FHWA, Freeway Management Handbook (on CD), 1998

FHWA, Incorporating ITS Into Transportation Planning: Phase 1 Final Report, 1997

FHWA, Integrating Intelligent Transportation Systems Within the Planning Process: An Interim Handbook, 1998

Gary-Chicago-Milwaukee ITS Priority Corridor, GCM Program Plan Update, July 1997

Georgia DOT, Incident Management Handbook, 1996

Houston TranStar, Freeway Incident Management Plan and Procedures, 1996

I-95 Corridor Coalition, Business Plan, 1998

ITS America, Strategic Plan for IVHS in the United States, 1992

Kentucky Transportation Cabinet, I-65 Freeway Incident Management Study, 1995

Koehne, J., F. Mannering, M. Hallenbeck, J. Nee, Washington State Transportation Commission (DOT), Framework for Developing Incident Management Systems (Revised), 1995

Metro Detroit Incident Management Coordinating Committee, Blueprint for Action, 1993

Mitretek for FHWA, Developing Freeway & Incident Management Systems Using the National ITS Architecture, 1998

Mitretek for USDOT, Intelligent Transportation Systems Benefits—1999 Update, 1999

Rush, J, (Parsons Brinkerhoff), M. Penic (SAIC), Integrating ITS and Traditional Planning—Lessons Learned I-64 Corridor MIS, 1998

TransCore (SAIC) for FHWA, Integrating ITS within Transportation Planning Process (Handbook), 1998

Virginia DOT, Smart Travel Program Activities in VDOT, 1997

Virginia DOT, VDOT Smart Travel Business Plan 1997-2006, 1997

Virginia Transportation Research Council & Old Dominion University, Final Report: Evaluation of the ITS Planning Process, 1995

Washington State DOT/ Washington State Patrol, WSDOT/WSP Interagency Joint Operation Policy Statement (DRAFT), November 1998

Wisconsin DOT/FHWA, 90/94 ITS Inter-city Corridor Study: Strategic Deployment Plan, 1996

For further information, contact:

Federal Highway Administration Resource Centers

Eastern Resource Center
10 S. Howard Street
Suite 4000 – HRC-EA
Baltimore, MD 21201
Telephone 410-962-0093

Southern Resource Center
61 Forsyth Street, SW
Suite 17T26 – HRC-SO
Atlanta, GA 30303-3104
Telephone 404-562-3570

Midwestern Resource Center
19900 Governors Highway
Suite 301 – HRC-MW
Olympia Fields, IL 60461-1021
Telephone 708-283-3510

Western Resource Center
201 Mission Street
Suite 2100 – HRC-WE
San Francisco, CA 94105
Telephone 415-744-3102

Federal Transit Administration Regional Offices

Region 1
Volpe National Transportation Systems Center
Kendall Square
55 Broadway, Suite 920
Cambridge, MA 02142-1093
Telephone 617-494-2055

Region 2
Alexander Hamilton Federal Building
1 Bowling Green, Room 429
New York, NY 10004
Telephone 212-668-2170

Region 3
1760 Market Street, Suite 500
Philadelphia, PA 19103-4124
Telephone 215-656-7100

Region 4
Atlanta Federal Center
61 Forsyth Street, SW
Suite 17T50
Atlanta, GA 30303-3104
Telephone 404-562-3500

Region 5
200 West Adams Street
24th Floor, Suite 2410
Chicago, IL 60606-5232
Telephone 312-353-2789

Region 6
819 Taylor Street
Room 8A36
Fort Worth, TX 76102
Telephone 817-978-0550

Region 7
901 Locust Street, Suite 40
Kansas City, MO 64106
Telephone 816-329-3920

Region 8
Columbine Place
216 16th Street, Suite 650
Denver, CO 80202-5120
Telephone 303-844-3242

Region 9
201 Mission Street, Suite 2210
San Francisco, CA 94105-1831
Telephone 415-744-3133

Region 10
Jackson Federal Building
915 Second Avenue, Suite 3142
Seattle, WA 98174-1002
Telephone 206-220-7954

Regional Traffic Incident Management Programs

THIS DOCUMENT IS ONE IN A SERIES OF PRODUCTS THAT ADDRESS ITS ISSUES PERTINENT TO A VARIETY OF AUDIENCES

ELECTED AND APPOINTED OFFICIALS • SENIOR DECISION MAKERS
TRANSPORTATION MANAGERS • TECHNICAL EXPERTS

Representing:

STATES • CITIES • COUNTIES • TRANSIT PROPERTIES • TOLL AUTHORITIES
EMERGENCY SERVICE PROVIDERS • METROPOLITAN PLANNING ORGANIZATIONS
ADDITIONAL TRANSPORTATION STAKEHOLDERS

Products Available in This Series:

- **Benefits Brochures** quote how ITS technologies have benefited specific areas.

- **Technical Reports** include results from various Field Operation Tests.

- **Cross Cutting Studies** present current data from related ITS applications.

- **Implementation Guides** assist project staff in the technical details of implementing ITS.

- **Case Studies** provide in-depth coverage of ITS applications in specific projects.

ITS Topics Addressed in This Series:

- COMMERCIAL VEHICLE OPERATIONS
- EMERGENCY SERVICES
- ENABLING TECHNOLOGIES
- EMISSIONS MANAGEMENT
- FREEWAY AND ARTERIAL MANAGEMENT
- PLANNING AND INTEGRATION
- REAL-TIME TRAVELER INFORMATION
- TRANSIT, TOLL, AND RAIL MANAGEMENT
- WEATHER INFORMATION FOR TRAVELERS AND MAINTENANCE

FOR A CURRENT LISTING OF AVAILABLE DOCUMENTS, PLEASE VISIT OUR WEB SITE AT:
www.its.dot.gov

INTELLIGENT TRANSPORTATION SYSTEMS

U.S. Department of Transportation
400 7th Street, SW
Washington, DC 20590

Federal Highway Administration
Room 3416, HOIT-1
Phone: (202) 366-0722
Facsimile: (202) 493-2027

Federal Transit Administration
Room 9402, TRI-10
Phone: (202) 366-4991
Facsimile: (202) 366-3765

FHWA-OP-01-002   EDL # 13149   FTA-TRI-11-00-03

www.ingramcontent.com/pod-product-compliance
Lightning Source LLC
Chambersburg PA
CBHW081855170526
45167CB00007B/3026